The Acts Of The Martyrdom Of Perpetua And Felicitas: The Original Greek Text Now First Edited From A Ms. In The Library Of The Convent Of The Holy Sepulchre At Jerusalem

James Rendel Harris, Seth K. Gifford

Nabu Public Domain Reprints:

You are holding a reproduction of an original work published before 1923 that is in the public domain in the United States of America, and possibly other countries. You may freely copy and distribute this work as no entity (individual or corporate) has a copyright on the body of the work. This book may contain prior copyright references, and library stamps (as most of these works were scanned from library copies). These have been scanned and retained as part of the historical artifact.

This book may have occasional imperfections such as missing or blurred pages, poor pictures, errant marks, etc. that were either part of the original artifact, or were introduced by the scanning process. We believe this work is culturally important, and despite the imperfections, have elected to bring it back into print as part of our continuing commitment to the preservation of printed works worldwide. We appreciate your understanding of the imperfections in the preservation process, and hope you enjoy this valuable book.

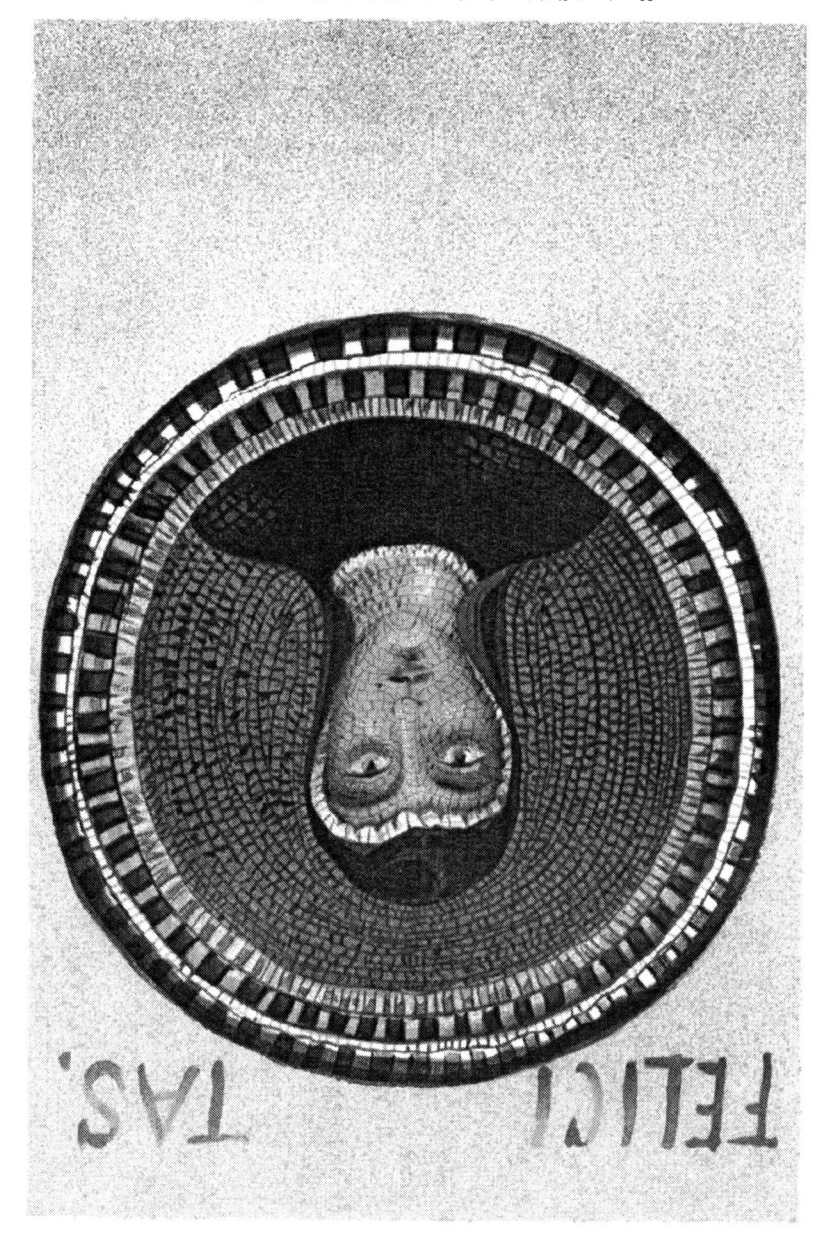

Mosaic of Felicius in the Archbishop's Palace, Ravenna.
Copied from the original by Edward Backhouse.

THE ACTS OF THE MARTYRDOM

OF

PERPETUA AND FELICITAS.

London: C. J. CLAY AND SONS,
CAMBRIDGE UNIVERSITY PRESS WAREHOUSE,
AVE MARIA LANE.

Cambridge: DEIGHTON, BELL AND CO.
Leipzig: F. A. BROCKHAUS.

THE ACTS OF THE MARTYRDOM

OF

PERPETUA AND FELICITAS;

THE ORIGINAL GREEK TEXT

NOW FIRST EDITED FROM A MS. IN THE LIBRARY
OF THE CONVENT OF THE HOLY SEPULCHRE
AT JERUSALEM

BY

J. RENDEL HARRIS,

FORMERLY FELLOW OF CLARE COLLEGE, CAMBRIDGE,
AND NOW PROFESSOR OF BIBLICAL LANGUAGES AND LITERATURE IN
HAVERFORD COLLEGE.

AND

SETH K. GIFFORD,

PROFESSOR OF GREEK IN HAVERFORD COLLEGE, PENNSYLVANIA.

LONDON:
C. J. CLAY AND SONS,
CAMBRIDGE UNIVERSITY PRESS WAREHOUSE.
1890

Cambridge:
PRINTED BY C. J. CLAY, M.A. AND SONS,
AT THE UNIVERSITY PRESS.

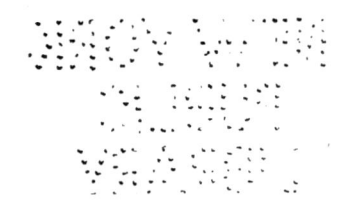

INTRODUCTION.

A new version of the Acts of Perpetua and Felicitas.

IN the following pages the reader is presented with what we believe to be the original Greek text of the celebrated Acts of the Martyrdom of Perpetua and Felicitas, the most beautiful as well as the most undisputed of all the early Christian martyr-records. These Acts have long been current in a Latin dress, but their language was often so obscure that it was not easy to extract a satisfactory meaning from the text, and there were many transliterated Greek words in their pages which must have seemed to scholars as not sufficiently accounted for by the fact that North Africa at the end of the second century was bilingual, or rather trilingual, and that of the languages spoken and written the Greek was perhaps as much the accepted speech as either the Latin or the Punic. Hence the suggestion became thrown out that the published Acts were probably, either wholly or in part, a translation from some lost Greek document. Such a document is now published, as copied by one of the editors from a volume of Lives of the Saints in the library of the Patriarch of Jerusalem. We shall discuss presently the evidence and give the arguments for believing that all existing Latin copies of the Acts are derived from this. At present it is sufficient to say that whether the Greek version be the primary or secondary fountain of the text, it is of such value for the understanding of it and for the clearing of its obscurities, that the welcome which it will meet from Patristic scholars will be sure to outweigh any blame that may attach to our unworthy presentation of it.

Of the Martyrs of Thuburbo.

Few Christians read the story of the martyrdom of Perpetua and her companions, or the almost contemporary story of the martyrs of Lyons and Vienne, without entering into sympathy with the exaltation of spirit which characterises these narratives, and which makes our writer break out into the concluding words "O most brave and blessed martyrs! O truly called and elected to the glory of Christ!" As the faithful, and yet not unartistic editor of the Acts pourtrays the glorious history of their struggle, the martyrs' faith, even after the lapse of nearly seventeen centuries, is still potent to reproduce in those that have ears to hear (and what Christian has not ears to hear such a story!) a longing after the constancy and the courage of earlier days. As we watch them ascend their brazen ladder, bristling on either side with sword points, into Paradise, they seem to turn, as Perpetua in her vision saw Saturus turn who had preceded her in the ascent, and say as he said, "We wait for thee." Their farewell is an endless welcome to later Christians. Something of the spikenard and balm and frankincense whose sweetness they breathe drops into our atmosphere, to make their memories always to be to the Church an acceptable savour of God in Jesus Christ. It is proper and right, therefore, to make the study of these recovered Greek Acts serve for our own emending as well as for that of the Latin text. And if as we read the record of Perpetua's more than manly wrestlings, we find ourselves rather to be in the place of the spectators than in the arena with the saints; in the historical succession of observation and criticism only, and not in the sequence of suffering with them for Christ in our day and generation, those brave eyes and that cloudless brow may well render us abashed with something of the shame wherewith she struck the spectators in the amphitheatre at Carthage. Thus she being dead may speak to us yet in exhortation or unto edification and comfort.

But the careful Christian student will not omit to note that both of these martyrdoms, the Thuburbitan martyrs and the other group to which we referred above (those of the Church in Gaul), are Montanist martyrdoms, and so are especially concerned with the personality and the operations of the Paraclete. So that when we say 'O most blessed martyrs,' we must go on and say 'O most blessed Paraclete'; for these martyrs are martyrs of the Holy Ghost, martyrs, that is, of the Living God considered not merely in opposition to the dead gods of the heathen, but as He lives and works in the saints. Now the works of the Holy Ghost are great, and are sought out of them that take pleasure therein.

Accordingly the redactor of the Acts instructs us to regard the grace of the Spirit as operating in two ways; first in the imparting of visions, the effect of which gift is that the Church receives a continual accretion to the deposit of revealed truth; and secondly in the raising up of martyrs, that is, in a continual increment of the testimony to the deposited verities of the kingdom of Christ: the advantage, then, which is to be derived from the story of the martyrs of Thuburbo is that they furnish very beautiful illustrations of both of these methods of the Divine operation. Nowhere are there recorded such instructive and striking visions; never were gathered into the great world-battle so fair a company of athletes whose triumph should belong to the clearest and most convincing chapter of the Christian evidences.

But there is another thing to be noted in connexion with these martyrdoms. We may say of martyrdom, in general, that it is something more than one of God's chosen ways of attesting the revelation which He has given; it is also in many cases an attestation that this truth has taken form in a society, which is interpenetrating and leavening all other society and slowly quickening it into higher forms; a society never more than half-visible, especially when, as in the present case, the living functions belong to the ecclesia within the ecclesia rather than to the ecclesia itself: a society whose constitution runs counter to the stratification of the outer world; where the mighty drop at their first faith from the thrones, and the miserable rise spontaneously into seats of power; until, re-organized in the kingdom of God, bond and free, rich and poor, male and female stand together in the beautiful spiritual brotherhood, of which Christ had spoken when He was upon earth.

The arena at Carthage presents this form of evidence in a most convincing manner, when there are gathered in it a company which have come together, so to speak, from the North and South, from the East and West, of human society; the noble Perpetua, the slaves Revocatus and Felicitas, and their other companions, we see them suffer in common for a common faith; but especially we may observe them as they are dragged back, after their fight with the beasts, from the gateway of the arena which is called the Vivific Gate, in order that under the dagger of the confector they may be dismissed through the real gate of Life already turning on its golden hinges; and grouping themselves together for one more saintly picture, they press from lip to lip the farewell kiss of Christian peace, in order that, as their historian says, they might perfect their testimony to the faith by the proper rite of the faith. And this kiss of faith and peace and charity, upon which they die, is the true monument and token of the revolution which God was accomplishing in the earth.

Supplementing then the statements of the martyrologist by this single consideration, that their martyrdom is a testimony to the existence of the Church on earth as well as to the truth for which the Church exists, we may pass on very briefly to answer the inevitable question in all martyrology, "What are these, and whence came they?"

> "What are these that shine from far?
> These that look over the golden bar?
> Strong as the lion, pure as the dove."

The Acts inform us that these martyrs come from Thuburbo Minus, a town not far from Carthage: indeed we have every reason to believe that they were removed to Carthage not long after their apprehension by the authorities: for it can hardly be of any other amphitheatre than Carthage that the writer is speaking, as being near the military camp, and apparently well furnished with wild beasts for the shows[1]. The period of the martyrdom is the year 203 A.D., when games are being celebrated in honour of the birthday of Geta Caesar. If we may accept the Greek date for the martyrdom (Feb. 2) then the date of their apprehension must be some weeks earlier than this.

The persons apprehended were Saturninus and Secundus; Revocatus and Felicitas, together with Vibia Perpetua. Their number was increased shortly after by the voluntary surrender of Saturus the deacon, who was absent when the law was first set in motion against them; but it was diminished before the games by the death of Secundus in prison, as often happened with early

---

[1] If not Carthage, we should naturally think of Theveste as the Roman military centre.

Christian martyrs when cast into stinking dungeons, and tortured in the interim between their apprehension and final condemnation.

All of them seem to have been young; Saturus from his office may perhaps be reckoned so: of the rest we are expressly told that they were young catechumens. Revocatus and Felicitas were fellow-slaves, and may have been brother and sister. Perpetua was about 22 years old, of noble birth and excellent education. It does not appear that any of them, except of course Saturus, were baptized at the time when they first came under suspicion; but in the interval during which they remained at large they were baptized. Perpetua's family seem to have been, on the whole, in sympathy with her; and one of her brothers was, like herself, a catechumen: but her father was bitterly opposed to her purpose and by an alternation of threats of violence with pathetic appeals did his best to divert her from her resolution[1].

Both of the women, Perpetua and Felicitas, were married: Perpetua was already a mother; Felicitas became so in the prison: but neither of the husbands appears in the story of the trial: it is not unreasonable, therefore, to suppose that they were concerned in the informations laid against the women; indeed, it is quite likely that, in a Montanising Church like that at Thuburbo, the women had deliberately left their husbands for the Gospel's sake. In any case it would be extremely improbable that both the husbands of two such very young women should have been dead at the time of the martyrdom: and indeed there is almost direct evidence in our Acts that the women had left their husbands; for when they come into the arena an attempt is made to array them as priestesses of Ceres: now we know from Tertullian that it was the custom in Africa for women to leave their husbands in order to dedicate themselves to the service of the goddess. Nor shall we be exercising our imagination unduly if we say that the proposal to dress the martyrs as priestesses of Demeter originated in the idea that it was an appropriate garb for women who had left their husbands for religious reasons. Such conduct was common to the Montanists and to the worshippers of Demeter: one of the charges levelled at Montanus by Apollonius (who wrote against the Cataphrygians at the end of

[1] Augustine by some misunderstanding makes Perpetua's mother as much opposed to her as was her father.

the second century) is that he had taught the dissolution of marriage[1]; and on the other hand, as intimated above, we have the direct and contemporary evidence of Tertullian with regard to the worship of the African Demeter: "we know," says he, "that widows attend upon the African Ceres, allured from their marriage by a most hard forgetfulness. For not only do they quit their husbands yet remaining alive, but even introduce other women to them in their own place (they no doubt smiling on it), refusing themselves all contact, even to the kiss of their sons[2]."

The Acts do not furnish us with a great deal of historical information beyond what bears on the incidents of the prison and the arena. Thus we find out that Dinocrates the other brother of Perpetua had died some years previously of a gangrene in his face; but we only find this out, because one of Perpetua's visions is concerned with his suffering in the next world, and his delivery therefrom by a sister's prayers.

We also learn that the bishop Optatus and presbyter Aspasius (who must be real persons) were not in much esteem with the martyrs nor with one another. There were factions in the Church, though upon what ground of division, whether Montanism or not, it is hard to say. But this information only leaks out from a vision of Saturus when after being caught up into Paradise, they find the bishop and presbyter shut out from the sacred Presence and ominously placed on the left-hand. In the same way we gather incidentally the names of others who had perished either in an earlier stage of the same persecution, or in an earlier persecution.

The fact is the writer was not furnishing materials with a view to history, for even the martyrdom is subservient to the visions; he relates nothing or next to nothing of the judicial proceedings, over which martyrologists are usually diffuse. But he had in hand two precious documents: one containing a vision seen by Saturus, the other containing three visions of Perpetua concluding with the intimation that 'who wills may tell the rest of the story.' Accordingly he told the martyrdom out of respect to Perpetua and as a fitting tribute to the inspiration of her visions. And indeed it is the visions that have impressed the Church, both Montanist and Catholic. The vision of the redemption of

---

[1] οὗτός ἐστιν ὁ διδάξας λύσεις γάμων Euseb. *H. E.* v. 18.
[2] *Tert. ad Uxorem* i. 6, *et de exhort. cast.* 13.

Dinocrates after death has probably as much to do with Perpetua's canonization as her death itself. Aubé was inclined to believe that the Acts were not really of this compound character; but that the writer had been guilty of an innocent literary forgery. He imagined he detected the same style in the language of the whole book. Of course this was not surprising if as Aubé suggested the Latin Acts were a translation from the Greek; only in that case he ought not to have projected the translator's uniformity of speech back upon the original scribes. The question can only be decided from the Greek version itself. Our own impression is that the differences of style are quite sufficient to discriminate the various hands in the book; or, if this be too strong, the uniformity of style is not sufficiently pronounced to invalidate the repeated statements of the redactor that he was using Perpetua's own materials.

Now when we turn to the story we find that, besides the historical notes that can be made from point to point, there are a multitude of little details concerning the Church life of the time, which are of the highest value. These Acts are an open window into the Church of the second century. Nevertheless we have not thought it best to discuss them at length nor to recapitulate the story, which we give both in the Greek and in the Latin, to say nothing of a shorter and later form of the Acts of the Martyrdom. We can not tell the actual story better than Perpetua tells it herself; and we have no right to tell it worse. Nor have we occupied space in proving over again what has so often been shewn as to the essentially Montanist character of the Acts. A few foot-notes will probably suffice on this point. The fact is that the changed attitude of modern theologians towards these assumed early heretics renders it unnecessary to revive old controversies. We can hardly deny their history when we have all agreed to build and adorn their sepulchres, as indeed the Western Church did so many centuries since. We therefore proceed to the few critical points that may require to be made, some of which have been already assumed in the preceding statements[1].

[1] For the copies of the Ravenna Mosaics of Perpetua and Felicitas which adorn this book, we are indebted to the kindness of our friend Catharine Backhouse, of Sunderland, who has given us leave to use the plates made from the drawings of her late husband for the illustration of his Church History.

On the Date of the Martyrdom.

A close approximation may be made to the year of the martyrdom by means of the external testimonies to the currency of the Acts and the internal allusions to historical personages. Thus we find not only that the Acts are referred to by Augustine in his commentary on the Psalms and elsewhere, but that they were even known to Tertullian. The latter father, in his treatise *De Anima*, refers to the visions of Perpetua, and in so doing he makes a mistake and gives us quotations from the vision of Saturus. It is fair, then, to infer that in Tertullian's mind the two visions were very closely bound up together, which probably means that he had used the written Acts, in which they are given in juxtaposition. This would make the Acts as well as the martyrdom earlier than the treatise *De Anima*.

But second, in Tertullian's tract against Scapula, mention is made of the very Hilarian who condemned our martyrs; for surely the 'Hilarianus praeses,' under whose administration a popular outcry was made against the Christians, can hardly be any other than the vice-proconsul of the Acts. So that we must place the martyrdom earlier than the treatise *ad Scapulam*. But this treatise bears every mark of having been written when Scapula was in office or very soon after; for Tertullian says "We battle with all your cruelty...we have sent you this letter as fearing not for ourselves but for you[1]." It is evident that this language implies that Scapula was still in the place of power.

But from the fact that Scapula was consul in A.D. 195, coupled with the fact that the time between consulate and pro-consulate

---

[1] The treatise *ad Scapulam* is full of allusions to recent historical persons and events, some of which can be approximately dated. Thus we have Hilarian, Cincius Severus, Vigellius Saturninus &c. Amongst recent tokens of the Divine displeasure towards the city of Carthage, he enumerates a plague of waters, threatening fires which had hung over the walls of Carthage by night, portentous thunderings, and an eclipse or blackness equivalent to an eclipse which was especially noted at Utica. This darkness and the thundering are due probably to volcanic causes, for we find from Dion Cassius lxxvi. 2 (shortly after 202 A.D.), that Vesuvius was in flame and that there were mighty roarings (μυκήματα μέγιστα) audible as far as Dion's house at Capua. The fires which hang over Carthage are the Northern Lights, which Dion describes well in lxxvi. 4 (i.e. not long after A.D. 195). πῦρ αἰφνίδιον νυκτὸς ἐν τῷ ἀέρι τῷ πρὸς βορρᾶν τοσοῦτον ὤφθη, ὥστε τοὺς μὲν τὴν πόλιν ὅλην, τοὺς δὲ καὶ τὸν οὐρανὸν αὐτὸν καίεσθαι δοκεῖν.

at the end of the second century is about 13 years, we should be inclined to place the pro-consulate of Scapula in Africa about the year 208 A.D. It has, however, been urged that in the treatise in question Severus is spoken of as if already dead: (e.g. c. iv. "Severus himself the father of Antoninus was mindful of the Christians"; "Severus...did not harm them":) so that it may be necessary either to depress slightly the above date for the pro-consulship of Scapula or for the time of production of the treatise; for Severus did not die until A.D. 211 (Feb. 4). In any case Hilarian must be a few years earlier than this.

Turning now to the Acts we find that Hilarian is deputy for a defunct proconsul, whose name is given in Latin as Minucius Timinianus and in Greek as Minucius Oppianus. Neither of these names has the right ring about it. We can find in Latin Minianus, Mucianus and the like, but not I think Timinianus. And the Greek form must either stand for Appianus or be a corruption from some more remote name. It is conceivable that Oppianus may stand for Apronianus who was consul in 191, and Timinianus for Septimianus who was consul in 190; or perhaps Septimianus might be the origin of both the names in question[1]. Unfortunately we cannot find that either of these was a Minucius. Septimianus is found written with various additional names in the inscriptions; sometimes M. Petronius Septimianus, and sometimes M. Sura Septimianus, so that his complete name should be M. Petronius Sura Septimianus. If either of these were the correct consul of the Acts we should have to look for the martyrdom about A.D. 203.

An examination of the seventy-sixth book of Dion Cassius which begins with the year 202 A.D. will shew that shortly after this time (see c. 8) Apronianus while in the government of the province of Asia was condemned while absent on a charge of treason. It would seem then that this consideration would rule out Apronianus from any place in our lists. As far as we can make out from the somewhat difficult style of narration of Dion Cassius, who is, however, here at his best as an eye-witness of almost all events which he records, this fixes the interval between the consulship and pro-consulship of Apronianus at twelve or thirteen years. And this will serve as a guide in determining the

---

[1] Thus TIM / CEΠIANOC } will easily give both OΠIANOC and TIMIANOC.

place of the African proconsuls in the Fasti. It points at all events to Septimianus or some suffect consul of the same period with him.

Now this date would agree very well with the plural form which we find in Hilarian's request to the prisoners to sacrifice for the welfare of the emperors, since at that time both Severus and Caracalla were Augusti; and it would agree also with the statement that the games were being celebrated in honour of Caesar's birthday, the Caesar in question being either Geta the brother of Caracalla, (murdered by the latter in A.D. 212), or else the term is used loosely of some festival connected with the birth or accession to power of the Augusti. The Latin text gives Geta Caesar definitely and it might almost be thought that this was sufficient evidence upon which to correct the Greek text and to base the chronology. If the birthday in question be the natural birthday it cannot be that of Severus, for he was born on the 11th of April, which will not agree with either the Latin or the Greek day for the commemoration of the martyrs (Feb. 2, Feb. 5, March 5). Neither can it be the birthday of Caracalla which was either the 4th or the 6th of April. The birthday then of Geta may perhaps be taken as the festival. A question however arises whether this be his natural birthday or the commemoration of his being made Caesar. Now the latter title was given him under the influence of the army at the time when Caracalla was made Augustus, which seems to have been in A.D. 198, and it is therefore urged that the festival in question may be the fifth anniversary of the Caesarship of Geta[1]. His natural birthday would seem to be excluded by the date (vi. Kal. Iun.) assigned to it by Spartian. In any case the story reads very well by the light of events of the year 202 or 203 A.D.

One other consideration may be given, which perhaps will be thought an artificial one; as we read our Acts, we shall be struck with the prominence given to the "kiss of peace" as a Christian sign and as a part of the Christian worship. It appears in the vision of Saturus where the prayer made before the throne is

[1] But Geta appears in official documents as Augustus at least as early as 204 A.D. This may be seen from a Fayûm papyrus (No. 1429, cf. *Mittheilungen aus der Sammlung der Papyrus Erzherzog Rainer*, Bd. ii. p. 13) which is dated as follows: Lιβ αυτοκρατορων καισαρων λουκιου σεπτιμ σεουηρου ευσεβους περτιν αραβικου αδιαβηνικου παρθικου μεγιστου και μα αυρηλιου αντωνινου ευσεβους και πουβλιου σεπτιμιου γετα καισαρος σεβαστων μεχειρ ιη.

concluded by the 'making of peace,' i.e. by the kiss of charity: it appears also in the pathetic closing scene where the martyrs expire in the arena: and the narrator adds the significant words that it was done in order that they might perfect the mystery of the faith by the rites proper to the faith. At first sight it seems a little artificial to imagine any polemical tendency in such an event at such a time; but that there should be something of a polemical character at all events in the interpretation given by the writer would not surprise any one who had noted the degree in which the Montanist ideas permeate the whole story: after "bread and cheese" in Paradise, and the bishops on the left-hand, we may be prepared for anything. Now it is a fact that precisely at the period in Church History to which our Acts refer, there was a dispute as to whether the "kiss of peace" was at all times proper, and whether there were not occasions when it was of the nature of true religion to omit it. And Tertullian (*De Oratione* c. xviii) in treating of this very question affirms that if the "Peace" is omitted the prayer is not perfected. The striking coincidence of this sentiment with the language of our Acts, "perfecting the mystery of the faith by the proper rite of the faith," should be noted, as it gives us light upon our text and upon its interpretation. It is pretty certain that we must read $\mu\nu\sigma\tau\acute{\eta}\rho\iota\sigma\nu$ with the Greek against the *martyrium* of the Latin, although the Latin translator has understood what was meant by $o\grave{\iota}\kappa\epsilon\acute{\iota}\omega\nu$ $\tau\hat{\eta}\varsigma$ $\pi\acute{\iota}\sigma\tau\epsilon\omega\varsigma$, and has given us the appropriate interpretation "sollemnia pacis," where *pax* stands again for the kiss.

Looking into the matter a little more closely we find that the difficulty arose in the following manner. The Church kept two station-days or sentry-days in the week, the Wednesday and Friday fasts. Now these fasts are of very early origin and probably arose out of antagonism to the Jewish bi-weekly fasts[1]; but as time went on, an explanation of their origin was given (which may indeed be the true one), viz. that these were the days when the Bridegroom was taken away, the Betrayal day and the Crucifixion day, and therefore they were the proper days for fasting. The question then came up, whether on these sentry-days the kiss of peace should be given, and it is certain that the Christian Church was divided on the point. Wednesday was an especially difficult day because on that day, the day of betrayal, Judas comes

---

[1] Cf. *Teaching of Twelve Apostles*, c. viii.

into prominence who betrayed the Lord with a kiss. But the difficulty seems to have been felt both with regard to the two weekly fasts and the annual fasts. One school urged that to give the "peace" was to break up the "station": another that to deny the "peace" was to leave the service imperfect. And it has been maintained that the Montanists, who wished for longer fasts and more of them, used this method of protesting against the Catholic laxity; it is said that they would prolong the fast by denying the peace. Those who have reflected on the fundamental conservatism of the Montanist movement will however be more disposed to believe that it was a Catholic innovation to deny the kiss of peace[1]. How widely this dispute spread may perhaps be judged by the traces of it in our own folk-lore, for it is clearly the basis of Launce's humorous description of his lady-love; "she is *not to be kissed fasting*—on account of her breath[2]."

Now it is well within the bounds of possibility that the writer of our Acts is alluding to this dispute and vindicating the giving of "peace" by the martyrs: and if this were the case then there would be some reason why they should have been incapable of the "peace" in the eyes of the severer critics: in other words it must have been either Wednesday or Friday. Friday may be excluded, first, because there is not much chance that such a coincidence between our Lord's suffering and his martyrs would have passed unnoticed; secondly, because there is, as stated above, a greater objection to the kiss of peace on Wednesday than on Friday. Now it is a matter of interest that Feb. 2, the Greek day of the martyrdom, was a Wednesday in the year 203 A.D.

One other point may be noted in connexion with the dating of the consuls and of the martyrdom. It has been felt that there was something unusual in the replacement of a proconsul by a local procurator: may we not go further and say that there is something strange in the proconsul dying in office, where the office is of such short tenure? And is there not a euphemism latent in the remark that the proconsul was recently deceased? When we reflect upon the number of persons of consular rank who were made away with by

---

[1] We may even go so far as to suspect that this 'Judas-kiss' is the ground of the tale told by the anonymous writer in Eusebius (*H. E.* v. 16) to the effect that Montanus died after the traitor's own manner (καὶ οὕτω δὲ τελευτῆσαι καὶ τὸν βίον καταστρέψαι Ἰούδα προδότου δίκην).

[2] Shakespeare, *Two Gentlemen of Verona*, Act III. Sc. ii.

Severus and Caracalla, it ought to surprise no one if a gap should occur in the list of candidates for the proconsulship, or a vacancy amongst those already elected. One has only to look at the lists, in Spartianus or Dion Cassius, of proscribed and assassinated nobles to feel the force of this. We have already intimated that Apronianus got into trouble with the emperor Severus. Spartian also records the death of Petronius, but places his murder subsequent to the death of Geta (A.D. 211). Whether this be Petronius Septiminianus or not, is hard to say; the narrative of Spartian is very confused and often returns on itself, sometimes slaying the slain over again under different emperors. We will content ourselves with saying that the dead proconsul of the Acts will probably be found amongst the political victims of Severus.

The relation of the Greek to the Latin Versions.

With regard to the shorter account, we shall elsewhere attempt to shew that it is independent of the other Latin version and probably based upon the Greek original. Additional force is given to this argument by the peculiarities of style noticeable in each. For example in the shorter version the connective *vero* occurs twenty times while *autem* is found but once. Ruinart's text has only three instances of *vero* while the use of *autem* is very frequent.

This seems also strong *prima facie* evidence in support of our second claim that Ruinart's text is a translation and that the Greek before us is the form in which the narrative was first written.

We shall not of course expect to find the Greek of the third century written by a Carthaginian who undoubtedly spoke some other language as his mother tongue entirely free from foreign idiom. We are prepared for certain peculiarities of style. Indeed it is not impossible that the author was more familiar with Latin than with Greek.

The passages which seem to point to a Greek original are scattered quite generally throughout the piece so as to leave no room for a bilingual theory.

The selections made for comparison are by no means equally convincing. The argument is from the nature of the case cumulative, so that a weak link does not necessarily invalidate the chain. On the other hand many points have been intentionally omitted which will appeal with different force to different individuals: the argument drawn from the choice and order of words, the arrangement of clauses, and the general sense of genuineness which pervades the Greek, will perhaps be the most potent factor in convincing the candid reader.

The examples which follow are taken in the order in which they occur, the Latin from Ruinart, side by side with the Greek.

III. Cum adhuc, inquit, cum persecutoribus essemus.	ἔτι, φησίν, ἡμῶν παρατηρουμένων.

The Greek evidently means "while we were still under suspicion," i.e. while they were still at large and their enemies were watching for an occasion to accuse them. For this use of παρατηρέω cf. Epis. Mart. Lugdun. 15, παντὶ δὲ τρόπῳ παρετήρουν ὡς μέγα τι κερδανοῦντες, εἰ μὴ τύχοιεν ταφῆς.

The Latin "while we were still with our persecutors" is at least a very curious way of saying what is expressed clearly and naturally by the Greek and what the context demands. And indeed the same remark applies to the next clause "Et me pater avertere et deicere pro sua affectione perseveraret," as compared with the simplicity and perspicuity of the Greek: ἐπεχείρει ὁ πατήρ μου λόγοις πείθειν με κατὰ τὴν ἑαυτοῦ εὐσπλαγχνίαν τῆς προκειμένης ὁμολογίας ἐκπεσεῖν.

Further on in the Chapter we may note the confusion of the Latin in the description of the prison, and especially where the prisoners are transferred to a ἡμερώτερον τόπον (Lat. meliorem locum) of the prison:

Tunc exeuntes de carcere universi sibi vacabant,	Καὶ δὴ ἕκαστοι προσαχθέντες ἐσχόλαζον ἑαυτοῖς,

as it is quite evident that they did not go out from the prison at this time.

At the beginning of Chap. IV. we have the following:

Tunc dixit mihi frater meus: Domina soror, iam in magna dignitate es, (et) tanta ut postules visionem...	Τότε εἶπέν μοι ὁ ἀδελφός, Κυρία ἀδελφή, ἤδη ἐν μεγάλῳ ἀξιώματι ὑπάρχεις τοσαύτη οὖσα, ὡς εἰ αἰτήσειας...

τοσαύτη οὖσα, translated into the Latin by *tanta*, has caused the confusion in the Latin MSS. One would naturally suppose that the writer would have avoided the ambiguity involved in *tanta* had he been writing Latin first hand.

In the next sentence *fidenter repromisi* is hardly the same thing as πίστεως πλήρης οὖσα ἐπηγγειλάμην, while the context clearly shews that fulness of faith rather than faithfulness was demanded.

Further on in the Chapter where the dragon presents his head quietly at the foot of the ladder, the action of fear is far more appropriately described than by the Latin, Et desub scala... lente elevavit caput.

In the next sentence the translator seems to have taken ὡς εἰς for ὡς εἰ rendering it *quasi* (Holstenius, Et quasi primum gradum calcassem, καὶ ὡς εἰς τὸν πρῶτον βαθμὸν ἐθέλησα ἐπιβῆναι).

In the passage beginning Chap. V.

Post paucos dies rumor cucurrit ut audiremur. Supervenit autem et de civitate pater meus, consumptus taedio, ascendit ad me, etc.	Μετὰ δὲ ἡμέρας ὀλίγας ἔγνωμεν μέλλειν ἡμᾶς ἀκουσθήσεσθαι· παρεγένετο δὲ καὶ ὁ πατὴρ ἐκ τῆς πολλῆς ἀποδημίας μαραινόμενος. καὶ ἀνέβη πρός με κτέ.

not to mention *ut audiremur*, the use of *supervenit* is striking as well as the position of *et* and the expression *de civitate*. The translator seems to have read ἐκ τῆς πόλεως for ἐκ τῆς πολλῆς and to have ignored the force of καί. Even if we could account for the first discrepancy on the supposition of the Latin original, the awkwardness of *et* with *de civitate* and the appropriateness of καί with ὁ πατήρ are certainly points in favor of the Greek. Again the mention of the father's return,—after speaking of his absence, Chap. III., ἀποδημήσαντος αὐτοῦ,—is much more in place than the meaningless phrase *de civitate*. Even if we assume that the prisoners had already been taken to Carthage it seems hardly likely that *de civitate* could refer to the father's coming from Thuburbo.

Chap. VI. begins as follows,—

Alio die cum pranderemus, subito rapti sumus ut audiremur.	Καὶ τῇ ἡμέρᾳ ἐν ᾗ ὥριστο ἡρπάγημεν ἵνα ἀκουσθῶμεν.

Is it possible that the translator has seen some form of ἀριστάω in ὥριστο? He has made quite as fatal mistakes elsewhere. But aside from this it is not probable that breakfast with the prisoners was so formal and protracted an affair that Perpetua, who in general makes little account of such trifles, would have thought the interruption of their meal worthy of special mention. It seems far easier to accept the other alternative and read "on the day appointed."

In the vision in which Perpetua sees her brother after his release and describes the fountain from which he drank, we have Chap. VIII.

Et piscinam illam quam retro videram, summisso margine usque ad umbilicum pueri; et aquam de ea trahebat sine cessatione, et super margine phiala erat aurea plena aqua: et accessit Dinocrates, et de ea bibere coepit, quae phiala non deficiebat. Et satiatus abscessit de aqua ludere more infantium gaudens, etc.	Καὶ ἡ κρηπὶς τῆς κολυμβήθρας κατήχθη ἕως τοῦ ὀμφαλίου αὐτοῦ, ἔρρεεν δὲ ἐξ αὐτῆς ἀδιαλείπτως ὕδωρ, καὶ ἐπάνω τῆς κρηπῖδος ἦν χρυσῆ φιάλη μεστή· καὶ προσελθὼν ὁ Δεινοκράτης ἤρξατο ἐξ αὐτῆς πινεῖν· ἡ δὲ φιάλη οὐκ ἐνέλειπεν· καὶ ἐμπλησθεὶς ἤρξατο παίζειν ἀγαλλιώμενος ὡς τὰ νήπια κτέ.

In the Latin, the use of *traho* for *haurio* is peculiar as well as the statement 'that he drank incessantly' standing, as it does, first; while the description proceeds 'Dinocrates approached and *began* to drink'; not incessantly, but until his thirst was quenched. Nor does the narrative allow us to take *trahebat* in a *general* sense of what D. was accustomed to do; for the vision only describes what Perpetua actually saw.

Finally we may notice the barbarism in *abscessit ludere*.

Turning now to the Greek we find that water was *flowing* from the fountain incessantly (the translator having read ἤρυεν for ἔρρεεν and taken ὕδωρ for the object), and that the boy, having drunk his fill, *began* to play (where ἤρξατο is taken for ἤρχετο).

For a similar description where the water is likewise flowing from the fountain, cf. Ruinart *Passio SS. Jacobi, Mariani et aliorum plur. Mart. in Numidia* c. VI., Sinus autem in medio pellucidi fontis exuberantibus venis, et plurimis liquoribus redundabat ...Tunc ibi Cyprianus phialam, quae super marginem fontis jacebat, arripuit; et cum illam de fontis rivulis implesset, hausit.

In Chap. X. near the beginning, *distinctam* can be traced pretty clearly to περιεζωσμένος, and in the next sentence, ποικίλα must mean 'of bright and varied colors' for which *multiplex* is a poor equivalent.

Further on in the Chapter in the description of the great βραβευτής we see how διεζωσμένος has again given rise to confusion in the Latin, from the fact that the translator has not governed the ἐσθῆτα by it nor placed πορφύραν in the relative clause.

In Chap. XI. we have the following:

Et liberati primam iam vidimus lucem immensam.	Καὶ δὴ ἐξελθόντες τὸν πρῶτον κόσμον φῶς λαμπρότατον εἴδομεν.

Cod. C gives a form much nearer the original than Ruinart's text, viz.: Et liberati primum iam mundo vidimus lucem immensam. It is evidently the ἐξελθόντες which has given the trouble and has been confused with some form of ἐλευθερόω.

In the next sentence *percepimus* is by no means an equivalent for μετειλήφαμεν, while the idea to be conveyed is undoubtedly that of *taking part* in the promise.

A few lines further on *via lata* seems in some mysterious way to represent ἀναλαβόντες τὴν ὁδόν.

Finally near the end of the Chapter the good Greek ἐζητοῦμεν δὲ καὶ περὶ τῶν λοιπῶν ποῦ ἄρα εἰσίν, has been mutilated into the Latin, Et quaerebamus ab (Holstenius et cod C, de) illis ubi essent ceteri.

In Chap. XII. how is the charming picture καὶ τῇ χειρὶ περιέλαβεν τὰς ὄψεις ἡμῶν marred in its Latin transformation, Et de manu sua traiecit nobis in facie (H, faciem); and on the other hand how supernaïve is 'go and play' for πορεύεσθε καὶ χαίρεσθε in the next sentence.

Near the middle of Chap. XIII. ἀναχωρέω has been given the meaning of ἀναχωρίζω, clearly counter to the sense of the passage.

In Chap. XVIII. we find διὰ τοῦτο τὴν ψυχὴν ἡμῶν παρεδώκαμεν rendered by *adeo animas nostras addiximus*: and in Chap. XX., near the end, ὃς παρειστήκει αὐτῇ by *qui ei adhaerebat*. The precision and correctness of the Greek seem evident in both cases.

For our last example let us compare a part of the account of the execution in Chap. XXI.:

Et cum populus illos in medium postularet, ut, gladio penetrante in eorum corpore, oculos suos comites homicidii adiungeret; ultro surrexerunt, et se quo volebat populus transtulerunt.	(Εἰς σφαγὴν δὲ) ὁ ὄχλος ᾔτησεν αὐτοὺς εἰς μέσον μεταχθῆναι ὅπως διὰ τῶν ἁγίων σωμάτων ἐλαυνόμενον τὸ ξίφος θεάσονται, καὶ μακάριοι μάρτυρες τοῦ χριστοῦ ἑκόντες ἠγέρθησαν, ᾐσχύνοντο γὰρ ὀλίγους μάρτυρας ἔχειν ἐπὶ τῷ μακαρίῳ θανάτῳ αὐτῶν· καὶ δὴ ἐλθόντων αὐτῶν ὅπου ὁ ὄχλος ἐβούλετο κτέ.

It hardly admits of doubt that the clause beginning ἠσχύνοντο, 'for they were ashamed to have only a few witnesses at their blessed death,' represents the original thought of the writer, for which apparently the Latin has the corrupt form 'oculos suos comites homicidii adiungeret.' At any rate the Latin is so badly muddled in this instance as well as in many others of which we have noted a few, that, on the assumption that it once had the correct form, it is difficult to understand how it could have lent so much perspicuity to the Greek and lost so much of that quality itself. For certainly several difficult and perplexing readings are entirely cleared up by reference to the Greek, while the Latin with its three MSS. very seldom throws any light on the Greek.

In the Latin text the following words are found apparently direct transcriptions from the Greek, with regard to which there seems no reason why they should have been chosen in place of genuine Latin words,—viz. machaera, tegnon, oramate, diastema, Hagios. In the Greek on the other hand we have πραιτώριον, ματρώνα, and the expression ἐν νέρβῳ (if indeed the text is correct) two of which are technical terms, where Latin words are most to be expected. An argument could hardly be drawn from these in favor of a Latin original.

Besides these *afa* is given for κονιορτός; the epithet *Optio* is applied to Pudens, the keeper of the prison, where Ruinart observes "Inspectorem putant Bollandiani a graeco verbo ὄπτομαι" (the word is wanting in the Greek); for the common use of this military term we refer to our note *in loc.*; and, lastly, *Cataractariorum* stands for τῶν παρατηρούντων.

As before stated the preceding argument makes no claim to exhaustiveness; on the other hand we believe that anyone who carefully compares the two texts will find much additional evidence in favor of the priority of the Greek.

On the shorter Acts of Perpetua and Felicitas.

We must now examine the relation which subsists between the shorter form of the Acts as published by Aubé from seven Latin MSS. in the National Library at Paris[1], and the longer Latin and Greek Acts respectively.

These Acts are valuable both for the history of the martyrdom and for the text of the longer form of the Acts. On any hypothesis as to the time of their production, they furnish in some respects new material to the historian; since they give us, for example, a complete account of the proceedings in court, and what constitutes properly the Acta of any given set of martyrdoms, viz. the interrogatories of the judge and the replies or confessions of the prisoners. Now this account may be mere matter of tradition written down to fill the evident lacuna in the current Acts, which are so taken up with the visions of the saints that they have no time left for the summary of the legal proceedings: or again they may be, as Aubé seems to think, the real record of the proceedings, modified only by some later hand, so as to refer them to the time of Valerian and Gallienus in whose consulate they place the martyrdoms[2]. It is merely a question of how much weight, less or more, should be given to the short form of the Acts when recording some details not given either in the longer Latin or Greek Acts.

When, however, the shorter Acts contain matter in common with the longer Acts, a little investigation shews that they do not constitute any fresh historical evidence, but, being derived from the longer form, the common matter is a new factor in the textual evidence where there is a diversity of readings, and in particular it becomes important to enquire whether the compiler of these Acts drew upon the Latin or Greek forms, respectively, of the longer work. Now in order to determine this point, the best way will be to place the parallel passages side by side, so that we may illustrate any passage in the shorter Acts by means of their possible or actual written sources. And this we may do as follows, taking the order from the shorter Acts:

[1] Aubé, *Les Chrétiens dans l'empire Romain*, pp. 521—525.
[2] Similar phenomena occur in the accounts of the martyrdom of Cyprian.

Short form.	Long form (Greek).	Long form (Latin).
Facta persecutione sub Valeriano et Gallieno Consulibus,	i. Ἐπὶ Οὐαλεριανοῦ καὶ Γαληνοῦ διωγμὸς ἐγένετο·	
Comprehensi sunt venerabiles viri iuvenes Saturus et Saturninus, duo fratres, Revocatus et Felicitas soror eius et Perpetua quae erat de nobili genere et habebat patrem et matrem et duos fratres et filium ad mamillam.	ii. Συνελήφθησαν νεανίσκοι κατηχούμενοι, Ῥευκᾶτος καὶ Φηλικητάτη συνδοῦλοι, καὶ Σατορνῖνος καὶ Σεκοῦνδος· μετ' αὐτῶν δὲ καὶ Οὐιβία Περπετούα, ἥτις ἦν γεννηθεῖσα εὐγενῶς... αὕτη εἶχεν πατέρα καὶ μητέρα καὶ δύο ἀδελφούς...εἶχεν δὲ καὶ τέκνον ὃ πρὸς τοὺς μασθοὺς ἔτι ἐθήλαζεν·	Apprehensi sunt adolescentes catechumeni, Revocatus et Felicitas conserva eius, Saturninus et Secundulus, inter quos et Vibia Perpetua, honeste nata...habens patrem et matrem et fratres duos...et filium infantem ad ubera.
Annorum enim erat illa duorum et viginti, apud Africam in civitate Tuburbitanorum.	Ἦν δὲ αὕτη ἐτῶν εἴκοσι δύο. Ἐν πόλει Θουβουρβιτάνων τῇ μικροτέρᾳ.	Erat autem ipsa annorum circiter viginti duorum.

Comparing the preceding passages we see (1) that the epitomator has apparently worked on a form of the Acts which already had the prefatory matter, and it is even conceivable from his using the words "apud Africam" that he used Acts which shewed also the Metaphrast's preface, (ἐν Ἀφρικῇ). The last point is, however, less certain.

(2) He seems to be interpreting a Greek text rather than the Latin; *comprehensi* for instance is a more literal rendering of συνελήφθησαν than the Latin *apprehensi*[1]. On the other hand *soror ejus* seems more like a correction of *conserva ejus* than a translation of σύνδουλοι. But then again, if he had been using a Latin text, he had no need to alter 'honeste nata,' nor 'ubera'; nor to drop the word 'circiter' in the Latin statement of the age of Perpetua.

(3) The historical data added are that Valerian and Gallienus were the *consuls*, and that, of the martyrs, Saturus and Saturninus were brothers, and Revocatus and Felicitas brother and sister. The last point is worked in again later on. We have no sufficient means of weighing the value of the statement.

Let us proceed with the comparison:

| Minutius proconsul dixit: | Καὶ Ἰλαριᾶνος ἐπίτροπος τότε τοῦ ἀνθυπάτου ἀποθανόντος Μινουκίου...λέγει. | Et Hilarianus procurator qui tunc loco proconsulis Minuci Timiniani defuncti...inquit. |

---

[1] Does the writer mean 'venerabiles' for an equivalent of κατηχούμενοι?

Here we have an arbitrary correction on the part of the redactor who, perhaps, did not think it correct that a proconsul's powers should be delegated to an inferior officer.

Perpetua vero dixit ad eum: Pater, ecce, verbi gratia, vides vas iacens aut fictile aut cuiuslibet generis?	Κἀγὼ πρὸς αὐτόν· Πάτερ, ἔφην, ὁρᾶς λόγου χάριν σκεῦος κείμενον ἢ ἄλλο τι τῶν τοιούτων;	Pater inquio vides verbi gratia vas hoc iacens, urceolum sive aliud?
Et ille respondit: Video, quid ad haec.	κἀκεῖνος ἀπεκρίθη· Ὁρῶ·	Et dixit: video.
Perpetua dixit, Numquid aliud nomen potest habere quam quod est? At ille respondit, Non. Perpetua dixit, Nec ego aliud nomen accipere possum quam quod sum, Christiana.	κἀγὼ· Ἄλλο ὀνομάζειν αὐτὸ μὴ θέμις; οὐδὲ δύναμαι εἰ μὴ ὃ εἰμί τούτεστιν χριστιανή.	Et ego dixi ei: numquid alio nomine vocari potest quam quod est? Et ait, Non. Sic et ego aliud me dicere non possum, nisi quod sum, Christiana.
Tunc pater eius audito verbo irruit super eam, volens oculos eius eruere: et exclamans confusus egressus est foras.	Τότε ὁ πατήρ μου ταραχθεὶς τῷδε τῷ λόγῳ ἐπελθὼν ἠθέλησεν τοὺς ὀφθαλμούς μου ἐξορύξαι· ἔπειτα μόνον κράξας, ἐξῆλθεν.	Tunc pater motus in hoc verbo, misit se in me, ut oculos mihi erueret: sed vexavit tantum et profectus est.

Here the short Acts have preserved the κράξας of the Greek, (=exclamans), which the Latin has corrupted somehow into vexavit. Confusus also in the last sentence is for the Greek ταραχθεὶς of which the Latin gives motus as the equivalent. We may, therefore, again recognize that the Greek is the primary authority.

But this being so, it becomes a question whether there was not some word in the first sentence after κείμενον, answering to the two Latin renderings fictile, and urceolum. And again whether the Greek should have restored to it the sentence corresponding to 'At ille respondit, non': 'et ait non.' In the last case the words 'et ait non' evidently break the sequence of the Latin: for there is in the longer Latin no et ego dixi to follow, as there should have been when the speaker had changed. Moreover the terse and striking Greek would be sure to have been expanded by the implied negative on the part of Perpetua's father.

The other question is not quite so clear: the Greek is quite intelligible but perhaps ἢ ὀστράκινον should be added.

Vidi in visu hac nocte scalam erectam mirabili altitudine usque ad caelum,	Εἶδον κλίμακα χαλκῆν θαυμαστοῦ μήκους· ἧς τὸ μῆκος ἄχρις οὐρανοῦ· στενὴ	Video scalam aeream mirae magnitudinis pertingentem usque ad caelum,

et ita erat angusta ut nonnisi unus per eam ascendere posset. Dextra vero laevaque inerant fixi cultri et gladii ferrei ut nullus circa se nisi ad caelum respicere posset.	δὲ ἦν ὡς μηδένα δι' αὐτῆς δύνασθαι εἰ μὴ μοναχὸν ἕνα ἀναβῆναι· ἐξ ἑκατέρων δὲ τῶν τῆς κλίμακος μερῶν πᾶν εἶδος ἦν ἐμπεπηγμένον ἐκεῖ ξιφῶν δοράτων ἀγκίστρων μαχαιρῶν ὀβελίσκων· ἵνα πᾶς ὁ ἀναβαίνων ἀμελῶς καὶ μὴ ἀναβλέπων τοῖς ἀκοντίοις τὰς σάρκας σπαραχθείη·	et ita angustam, per quam nonnisi singuli ascendere possent: et in lateribus scalae omne genus ferramentorum infixum. Erant ibi gladii, lanceae, hami, machaerae, ut si quis negligenter aut non sursum adtendens ascenderet, laniaretur et carnes eius inhaererent ferramentis.
Sub ea vero iacebat latens draco teterrimus ingenti forma, ut prae metu eius quivis ascendere formidet.	Ἦν δὲ ὑπ' αὐτῇ τῇ κλίμακι δράκων ὑπερμεγέθης ὃς δὴ τοὺς ἀναβαίνοντας ἐνήδρευεν ἐκθαμβῶν ὅπως μὴ τολμῶσιν ἀναβαίνειν.	Et erat sub ipsa scala draco cubans mirae magnitudinis qui ascendentibus insidias parabat et exterrebat ne ascenderent.
Vidi etiam ascendentem per eam Saturum usque ad sursum et respicientem ad nos et dicentem: ne vereamini hunc draconem qui iacet: confortamini in gratia Christi, ascendite et nolite timere ut mecum partem habere possitis.	Ἀνέβη δὲ ὁ Σάτυρος·... ὡς οὖν πρὸς τὸ ἄκρον τῆς κλίμακος παρεγένετο ἐστράφη καὶ εἶπεν.................	Ascendit autem Saturus prior:......et pervenit in caput scalae et convertit se ad me et dixit mihi..... ....
Vidi etiam iuxta scalam hortum ingentem, copiosissimum et amoenum et in medio horto sedentem senem in habitu pastorali et mulgentem oves, et in gyro eius stantem multitudinem candidatorum: et aspiciens ad nos vocavit ad se et dedit nobis omnibus de fructu lactis. Et cum gustassemus, turba candidatorum responderunt Amen: et sic prae clamore vocum sum expergefacta.	καὶ εἶδον ἐκεῖ κῆπον μέγιστον καὶ ἐν μέσῳ τοῦ κήπου ἄνθρωπον πολιὸν καθεζόμενον, ποιμένος σχῆμα ἔχοντα, ὑπερμεγέθη ὃς ἤλμευγεν τὰ πρόβατα· περιεστήκεισαν δὲ αὐτῷ πολλαὶ χιλιάδες λευχειμονούντων· ἐπάρας δὲ τὴν κεφαλὴν ἐθεάσατό με...... καὶ ἐκάλεσέν με καὶ ἐκ τοῦ τυροῦ οὗ ἤλμευγεν ἔδωκέν μοι ὡσεὶ ψωμίον· καὶ ἔλαβον ζεύξασα τὰς χεῖράς μου, καὶ ἔφαγον· καὶ εἶπαν πάντες οἱ παρεστῶτες· Ἀμήν. Καὶ πρὸς τὸν ἦχον τῆς φωνῆς ἐξυπνίσθην.	et vidi spatium horti immensum et in medio horti sedentem hominem canum in habitu pastoris, grandem, oves mulgentem: et circumstantes candidatos millia multa: et levavit caput et aspexit me:......... et clamavit me et de caseo quod mulgebat dedit mihi quasi buccellam, et ego accepi iunctis manibus et manducavi. Et universi circumstantes dixerunt Amen. Et ad sonum vocis experrecta sum.

A little examination will shew that the differences between the two Latin texts in those parts of the story which they have in common, are not due to free handling of the longer Latin on the part of the redactor of the shorter Acts: they are fundamental differences and not mere emendations. The originality of the shorter acts is shewn also by the use of peculiar expressions like 'in gyro eius,' 'de fructu lactis.' We should conclude then that both the Latin versions arise in some way out of the Greek. Dismissing, then, the longer Latin Acts, let us see how the compiler uses his Greek materials.

The text of the shorter Acts now proceeds with the judicial interrogatories; in which nothing seems to be taken from the published Acts, unless it be the information as to the condition of Felicitas, until we come to the trial of Perpetua.

Proconsul ad Perpetuam dixit: Quid dicis, Perpetua, sacrificas? Perpetua; Christiana, inquit, sum et nominis mei sequor auctoritatem ut sim Perpetua. Proconsul dixit: Parentes habes. Perpetua respondit, Habeo.	Ἐπίθυσον ὑπὲρ σωτηρίας τῶν αὐτοκρατόρων· κἀγὼ ἀπεκρίθην οὐ θύω.

This question appropriately makes way for the introduction of the scene in the court between Perpetua and her father; the compiler of the Acts now draws largely on the longer version. But in order to fill up obvious deficiencies in the story as received, the husband of Perpetua turns up with the rest of the family. He is, however, little better than a lay figure adding nothing to the dialogue ("the poor craven bridegroom says never a word") and only an imperceptible quantity to the tears and lamentations.

Audientes vero parentes eius, pater, mater, fratres et maritus simulque cum parvulo eius qui erat ad lac venerunt cum essent de nobili genere. Et videns eam pater eius stantem ante proconsulis tribunal cadens in faciem suam dixit ad eam: Filia, iam non filia, sed domina, miserere aetati meae patris tui si tamen mereor dici pater, miserere et matris tuae quae te ad talem florem aetatis perduxit, miserere et fratribus tuis et huic infelicissimo viro tuo, certe vel parvulo huic qui post te vivere non poterit.	Καὶ ἐφάνη μετὰ τοῦ τέκνου μου ὁ πατήρ· .... [ὁ πρὸς τοῖς μασθοῖς ἔτι...]¹ [γεννηθεῖσα εὐγενῶς] .... ῥίπτειν ἐπὶ γῆς καὶ πρηνὴς κατακείμενος... .... Θύγατερ...οὐκέτι με θυγατέρα ἀλλὰ κυρίαν ἐπεκάλει.. ἐλέησον τὰς πολιάς μου, ἐλέησον τὸν πατέρα σου, μνήσθητι ὅτι ταῖς χερσὶν ταύταις πρὸς τὸ τοιοῦτον ἄνθος τῆς ἡλικίας ἀνήγαγόν σε· .... ὅρα τοὺς ἀδελφούς σου........................ ἴδε τὸν υἱόν σου ὃς μετὰ σὲ ζῆν οὐ δύναται.
Depone hanc cogitationem tuam. Nemo enim nostrum post te vivere poterit, quin hoc generi meo nunquam contigit.	ἀπόθου τοὺς θυμούς·........................ οὐδεὶς γὰρ ἡμῶν μετὰ παρρησίας λαλήσει ἐάν τί σοι συμβῇ.

---

[1] Evidently the epitomator repeated these words from the earlier chapters.

A comparison between the two texts will shew that the compiler has recklessly displaced the sequence of the Greek Acts; the address of the father to Perpetua takes places in the open court; in fact two or three visits and addresses are tesselated together. At the end the word συμβῇ suggests the fact that no such shame has ever happened *to our family*.

Praecepit ut in Caesaris natale bestiis mitterentur.	Τότε ἡμᾶς πάντας πρὸς θηρία κατακρίνει· γενέθλιον γὰρ ἤμελλεν ἐπιτελεῖσθαι Καίσαρος.
Et cum essent in carcere iterum vidit visionem Perpetua Aegyptium quendam horridum et nigrum iacentem et volutantem se sub pedibus eorum............	Καὶ ἦλθεν πρός με Αἰγύπτιός τις ἄμορφος τῷ σχήματι μετὰ τῶν ὑπουργούντων αὐτῷ .... καὶ ἀντικρὺς βλέπω Αἰγύπτιον ἐκεῖνον ἐν τῷ κονιορτῷ κυλιόμενον...............
prostrato inimico generis humani.	πρὸς τὸν διάβολόν ἐστιν ἡ ἐσομένη μάχη.
Contristantibus vero iis de Felicitate quod esset praegnans in mensibus octo, statuerunt unanimiter pro ea precem ad Dominum fundere. Et dum orarent subito enixa est vivum. Quidam vero de custodibus dixit ad eam: Quid factura es cum veneris ad amphitheatrum quae talibus detineris tormentis?	ἐκείνη γάρ...ὀκτὼ μηνῶν ἔχουσα γαστέρα... Ἀλλὰ καὶ οἱ συμμάρτυρες αὐτῆς περίλυποι ἦσαν σφόδρα οὕτω καλὴν συνεργὸν... καταλείπειν...κοινῷ στεναγμῷ ἐνωθέντες προσευχὴν πρὸς τὸν Κύριον ἐποιήσαντο· καὶ εὐθὺς μετὰ τὴν προσευχὴν ὠδῖνες αὐτὴν συνέσχον· [ἔτεκεν δὲ κοράσιον] ἔφη δέ τις τῶν παρατηρούντων ὑπηρετῶν· εἰ νῦν οὕτως ἀλγεῖς τί ἔχεις ποιῆσαι, βληθεῖσα πρὸς θηρία;................
Felicitas respondit: Hic ego crucior, ibi vero pro me Dominus patietur.	Κἀκείνη ἀπεκρίθη· Νῦν ἐγὼ πάσχω ὃ πάσχω· ἐκεῖ δὲ ἄλλος ἐστὶν ὁ πάσχων.
Euntibus vero eis sequebatur Felicitas quae ex sanguine carnis ad salutem sanguinis ducebatur et de obstetrice ad gladium et de lavatione post partum balnei sanguinis effusione meruit delavari.	Ἠκολούθη δὲ ἡ Περπετούα...... Ὁμοίως δὲ καὶ ἡ Φηλικητάτη,...ἀπὸ αἵματος εἰς αἷμα, ἀπὸ μαίας πρὸς μονομαχίαν, μέλλουσα λούσασθαι μετὰ τὸν τοκετόν, βαπτισμῷ δὴ ὑστέρῳ.
Passi sunt sub Valeriano et Gallieno imperatoribus apud Africam in civitate Tuburbitanorum sub Minutio proconsule die nonarum Martiarum.	Ut supra. (The Latin date instead of the Greek.)
Actus eorum in ecclesia ad aedificationem legite, etc.	...οὐκ ἧσσον τῶν παλαιῶν γραφῶν ἃ εἰς οἰκοδομὴν ἐκκλησίας ἀναγινώσκεται κτέ.

Reviewing the manner in which the compiler of the shorter Acts has used (or misused) his materials, we can hardly feel confidence in any apparently fresh historical details which he gives. Nor can we suppose that the judicial interrogatories are anything else than a successful attempt to fill up an obvious lacuna in the history of the proceedings. We cannot agree with Aubé that they bear a decided stamp of genuineness: it is possible to fabricate a judicial investigation without making a ridiculous caricature of the judge. The fact that he is humane does not make the dialogue historical.

To sum up: the shorter Latin Acts were made, solely from the Greek, after the time of Valerian and Gallienus: and since they were made from a Greek MS. which already had erased the name of Geta, and prefixed the notice as to Valerian and Gallienus, we may conclude that they must have been written some time later than the middle of the third century. If the closing sentences belong to this version in its first form, as seems almost certain, then these Acts are posterior to the time when Perpetua and Felicitas were received into the Calendar (? Carthaginian or Roman), with the date of their celebration corrected from February to March. So that again we must ascribe them to a later date.

The compiler of the Acts has drawn nothing from the longer Latin version; and therefore, as far as he was concerned, these Latin Acts may be held not to have existed; a consideration which militates very strongly against the current belief in the antiquity of the published Latin text of Ruinart and Holstein.

On the influence of the Acts of Perpetua on the later Martyrologies.

It is a curious study to trace the manner in which one famous martyrdom acts upon the record of those that come afterwards, so that the genuine martyrologies copy the language of earlier recitals of a similar nature, and the apocryphal martyrologies intrude habitually not only the language but even historical details from genuine records, often without a pretence at disguise in the borrowed matter. And this tendency makes it often difficult to discriminate between true and false in a series of connected martyrdoms. For instance the martyrdom of S. Victor and his companions relates the crushing of the saint between mill-stones and makes him say in the midst of his tortures that he is "the wheat of God"; it is clear that the writer has borrowed this from the epistle of Ignatius to the Romans, where 'frumentum Dei' is merely a strong figure of speech; he has given us an incident in which the figure is very literally translated. Obviously

S. Victor never said anything of the kind; and it is probably almost as certain that he never suffered anything of the kind; but whether we can go further and detect the residual grains of truth out of the heap of fiction is more difficult. Ruinart prints the whole story, of course, without suspicion amongst his *Acta Sincera*; but then Ruinart used his winnowing fan very gently: and the critical breeze was only beginning to blow.

Lightfoot holds that the Acts of Perpetua are a case of the same kind inasmuch as they are coloured by the language of the Ignatian epistles, a proposition which we shall examine presently; but in this case, since it is only language that is borrowed and not history, no reflection is made upon the authenticity of the Acts. The same thing is true of a host of martyrdoms which furnish parallelisms with the great prae-Christian models of suffering endurance, such as the case of the Three Children in the Furnace, or the group of Maccabee Children. It is natural, for instance, for martyrs in the flames to see Christ with them, or to be seen with him; almost as natural for them to be refreshed with a whistling wind or a miraculous dew. But when the details of the hagiology present more decided coincidences than these simple subjective ones, we may easily find ourselves in the region of fable pure and simple. Such is the case for instance of the martyrdom of Felicitas and her seven sons which is nothing more than a Christian reprint of the heroism of the Maccabees.

It is natural, then, to expect that such a famous early martyrdom as that of Perpetua should have left its mark upon later stories: we will give one instance, with the view of shewing how closely one writer can attach himself to another without being suspected of plagiarism or worse.

The *Sincere Acts* of Ruinart contain the account of the Passion of Montanus, Lucius and other African martyrs. Ruinart refers these martyrdoms to the year 259 A.D. or 260.

The writer of these Acts is persuaded that modern examples of the faith may, under the influence of divine promise, touch the mark of earlier times: (c. IV. nec difficile credentibus fuit, nova posse ad vetera exempla pertingere, Domino per spiritum pollicente): a theme to which he returns at the close of the story, intimating that we may learn from the new scriptures as we have learnt from the old; (c. XXIII. "O martyrum gloriosa documenta! O testium Dei experimenta praeclara, quae ad memoriam posterorum scripta sunt merito, ut quemadmodum de scripturis veteribus exempla, dum discimus, sumimus; etiam de novis aliqua discamus"). Obviously the writer has been imitating the Acts of Perpetua. So far the imitation has nothing to do with his veracity; it is literary, not historical. But what are we to say when we find that they are brought before a Procurator who happens to be filling the place of a Proconsul who has died in office? c. VI. "subito rapti sumus ad Procuratorem qui defuncti proconsulis partes administrabat." In the Acts of Perpetua this has been one of the difficult points to explain, on account of the deficiency of precedent for such a delegation of proconsular power[1]. But even if precedent existed, the probability of this event happening in Africa twice in fifty years may be taken as infinitely small. Moreover the language "subito rapti sumus" is taken from the Perpetua Acts. When they come to the prison, instead of making the martyrs feel as Perpetua did "how dreadful and how dark was this place!" and then go on in faith until the prison becomes a palace, our writer plunges his prisoners into palatial joys at the start: they do not fear the foulness nor the gloom; the prison shines with the glory of the Spirit, c. IV. "nec expavimus foedam loci illius nec caliginem. Moxque carcer tenebrosus Spiritu perlucente resplenduit, etc." This last description might be merely an improvement upon Perpetua; but when we go a little farther, we find the governor of the prison trying to starve the martyrs, and we have moreover a series of visions which are evidently suggested by those in the Acts of Perpetua. It is true that he does not directly imitate the Dinocrates-vision, but when one of the women-martyrs sees her son who has suffered before her sitting by the margin of waters and hears him speak to her: when a youth of amazing stature enters with cups in his hands, the draught from which does not diminish the supply (quae phialae non deficiebant), we know that the story of Dinocrates was in the mind of the writer and that he made the best use he could of his materials.

We might point out many more coincidences, but these will probably be sufficient, to shew that the Acts of Montanus, Lucius and their company are a deliberate forgery, based chiefly upon the Acts of Perpetua and Felicitas.

---

[1] Marquardt (*Röm. Staatsverwaltung*, I. p. 415, n. 3) quotes these Acts in order to establish the precedent!

Tertullian and the Acta Perpetuae.

It has been frequently suggested that there is some relation between Tertullian and the author of the Acts of Perpetua, and coincidences of language have been pointed out between the writings of the great African father and our Latin text, so as to support the thesis that perhaps the Acts themselves come from the pen of Tertullian. Now it will be evident that, if our hypothesis of a Greek original be correct, these arguments lose almost all their force. It is not indeed impossible that Tertullian may have been the author of Greek Acts, but we have no evidence by which to support the theory in the shape of a comparison between what he is known to have written and what he may be maintained to have written. So that the theory falls to the ground. There is, however, one direction in which we may find traces of Tertullian which has not, as far as we know, been pointed out previously.

If we are right in referring the martyrdom to any time near 200 A.D., and to any place near Carthage, it is extremely difficult to believe that so valiant a defender of the faith as Tertullian had nothing to do for the martyrs and nothing to say about them. It would be almost impossible that such should have been the case if he had been a pronounced Montanist at the time of the martyrdom, and when we reflect upon the difficulty with which any of his writings, except a very few tracts, can satisfactorily be labelled non-Montanist, we are obliged to admit that the tide of sympathy with the new movement must have set in some time before what the orthodox church writers are pleased to call 'his fall.' Thus it is in the highest degree probable that Tertullian would have in some way or other shewn sympathy with the imprisoned brethren and sisters. So far we are only reasoning generally, and after an *a priori* manner: but when we turn to Tertullian's writings we find one tract addressed directly to a group of martyrs in prison, which is singularly applicable to the circumstances of Perpetua and her friends; so that it furnishes at least a commentary, if not a historical supplement to the story of their sufferings.

In the tract *ad Martyras* we have very few direct allusions by which to fix its date; nor is this surprising, when we regard the brevity of its composition. It has been regarded by some as amongst Tertullian's earliest works. This result is arrived at by the Oxford translators of Tertullian as follows: the tract belongs to a time of persecution; but no martyrs have already suffered, or they would have been named; therefore it is the commencement of a time of persecution. And since the closing words of the tract contain an encouragement to the martyrs on the ground that, even if they were not Christians, their lives would not necessarily be secure, as we see by the sudden removal of persons of all classes and conditions who have fallen under the condemnation of the government, it has been held that the tract refers to the suppression of the followers of Albinus and therefore to the year 197.

Now this reasoning is invalidated as regards the martyrs, first, because it has the usual weakness of an argument from silence, and secondly, because Tertullian does allude to previous martyrs in his opening remarks, where he says they have been in the habit of giving from their prison certificates of peace to lapsed members of the Church. But it is also weakened by the fact that the proscription and assassination of persons suspected by the government can hardly be held to have been ended in a single year; for the whole period with which we are concerned is rife with charges of treason. So that it does not seem necessary to put the date as far back as 197 A.D.

But now let us examine the tract a little more closely: and first we notice that it is divided into two parts by alternate addresses made to men and women. Thus in c. II. he addresses the martyrs as "blessed men," and so in the beginning of c. III. But in c. III. he changes the address from 'benedicti' to 'benedictae,' and it is clear that this need not be regarded as a copyist's error, since a little further on he brings in instances of female constancy such as Lucretia, in order that the blessed women might rival their own sex.

Now we conclude from this that the group of martyrs was composed both of men and women. But our Acts give no hint that women had suffered in the earlier part of the persecution with Iucundus, Artaxius and the rest. We should therefore be disposed to think that the women addressed were our own Perpetua and Felicitas. At all events they satisfy the condition.

But further the martyrs were many of them young, since Tertullian at the commencement of the second chapter says that there were some hindrances of the soul which had come after them just as far as *their parents* had, viz. to the prison door. Whether he means to include parents amongst the hindrances left behind, as in Perpetua's case, is not clear; but the language implies that there was a large juvenile contingent amongst the martyrs. Now our Acts emphasize especially the youthfulness of this band of Christian soldiers.

The form of Tertullian's sympathy is dictated by the trials present and prospective of the martyrs. He commiserates them on the darkness and foulness of their prison. We must not unduly press such an exactness of agreement with the language of the Acts, for it is probable that all prisons were much the same in regard to light and sweetness. But we may say it is language very adapted to our martyrs which can speak as follows: "the world containeth the greater number of criminals, to wit the whole race of man: it awaiteth moreover the judgment not of the *proconsul* but of God. Wherefore, blessed men, consider that ye have been translated from a prison to a place, it may be, of safe keeping. *It hath darkness*, but ye yourselves are lights. *It hath bonds*, but ye have been made free by God. *An evil breath* is uttered there; but ye are a sweet savour. *A judge is looked for*, but ye shall judge even the judges themselves." Could anything be more appropriate to the condition of the martyrs from Thuburbo than this?

In the same way he touches on the suffering of their legs in the stocks, on the probability of their having to run the gauntlet under the whips of the *venatores* and the like.

But the greatest piece of evidence of all consists in the directions which Tertullian gives them to tread the dragon under foot in his own house. "Let him flee from your sight and hide himself in his utmost recess coiled up and listless like a serpent that hath been charmed and fumigated away." Read this by the side of Perpetua's account of the way in which, at the name of Jesus, she saw the dragon retreat beneath the ladder, so that she trod upon his head as she began her ascent, and one will be disposed to say that either the story of the ladder and the dragon had come to Tertullian's ears, or that his words had furnished the raw material, if we may so express it, for the vision which Perpetua saw.

The way in which Tertullian works out the figure of the

athletic contest in which the martyrs are engaged is very remarkable, because it runs parallel in some points with Perpetua's wrestling match with the Egyptian. It is true that the illustration is a sufficiently common one, and therefore coincidences are not to be pressed as they are in the previous illustration; but at all events let us look at them. According to our Acts, then, the last vision of Perpetua is a vision of her wrestling with the devil under the form of an Egyptian. A most beautiful youth attended by a band of beautiful companions appears as her trainer. Presently there enters a man of marvellous height, robed in purple of more than ordinary dignity, and holding the judge's staff in his hand.

The Latin version, not seeing the necessity apparently both for the youth of amazing beauty and the judge of amazing stature, has left out the former, furnishing thus only a bevy of young men for backers of the athlete. But one suspects that both God and Christ are represented in the vision: God the judge of all and Christ the trainer of the faithful. And when we turn to Tertullian we find as follows: "ye are about to undergo a good fight wherein the president is the Living God: the trainer, the Holy Spirit: the crown, eternity: the prize, of angelic being, the citizenship of the Heavens: the glory, for ever and ever. Wherefore your Master Christ Jesus, who hath given you the unction of the Spirit, hath brought you forth into this wrestling ground etc." Now we should infer from this that the youth of amazing beauty is either Christ or the Holy Spirit: and thus we are able to justify the Greek text against the Latin, and to shew a second case in which Tertullian's language is strikingly like the fabric of Perpetua's visions.

We are disposed to think that these agreements are sufficient to prove that the tract *ad Martyras* was written to Perpetua and her companions shortly after their removal to the military prison at Carthage. We know nothing that is foreign to such a hypothesis except that there is a lapse of some five or six years between the dates that have hitherto been ascribed respectively to the tract of Tertullian, and the martyrdom. But these dates, and especially the former, have still some measure of uncertainty attaching to them. We propose, therefore, to lower the date of the *ad Martyras* by the necessary interval for agreement with the martyrdom of Perpetua.

On the relation of the Acts of Perpetua and Felicitas to the Ignatian Controversy.

The Acts of Perpetua and Felicitas have been brought into prominence in the great historical controversy as to the genuineness of the Ignatian epistles in two ways: first, to repel the charge of anachronism brought by Bochart against the epistle of Ignatius to the Romans on the ground of its use of the word "leopard[1]," when this word was an artificial and late word not found earlier than the time of Constantine, the proper Greek word being πάρδαλις: secondly, they have been employed to demonstrate the antiquity of the Ignatian epistles by means of actual quotations from those epistles, or of parallelisms in language amounting to quotations, which occur in the current Acts of Perpetua and her companions.

Now it is not our business, certainly not here and now, to write our views on the Ignatian controversy: but it is well within our province to test any of the links in the historical argument evolved by Pearson, Usher and Lightfoot for the defence of the Ignatian epistles, where the arguments are based upon the text of which we give, as we believe, the first and authoritative form. We shall accordingly say a few words on each of the two questions referred to above.

And first with regard to the "ten leopards" of Ignatius.

Bochart in his *Hierozoicon* says as follows: "Leopardi vox serius usurpari coepit, nempe Constantini aevo. Proinde Ignatii ad Romanos Epistola quam circumferunt, eo demum saeculo fuisse scriptam vel ex hoc argumento colligas, quod Leopardorum diserte meminit."

If we may believe Pearson (*Vindiciae Ignatianae* II. 92) Bochart based this observation on a remark of Gesner's. Pearson wittily remarks that it is quite possible that the word 'leopard,' does not exist in those Roman writers, earlier than the fourth century, who had been studied by Bochart; but there were other authors, of the period in question, whom Bochart had not read; some of them were no doubt lost, but there were extant a few authors who had used the word; "non legit, opinor, Bochartus, passiones SS. Perpetuae et Felicitatis primo in lucem ab Holstenio productam": he then quotes the numerous allusions to the

---

[1] Ign. *ad Rom.* v. "Bound to ten leopards" (λεοπάρδοις).

'leopard' in our Acts and observes that the Acts were written one hundred years before the time of Constantine. Upon which Lightfoot remarks (*Ignatius* I. 397): "It is sufficient to say that Pearson at once proved the extravagance of this assertion by producing an example of the word as early as Severus (A.D. 202), and thus convicting Bochart of an error of a whole century at all events. I have been able to carry the evidence much farther back."

Now we have the right to ask how the argument stands in the light of our recovered Greek Acts. If the Latin were the original, since there is, as far as we know, no suspicion that the text of the Passion is corrupt, then 'leopardus' is good Latin in the year 202 A.D.: and this means that it is possible in Greek long before the time mentioned by Bochart. But we have shewn that, so far from the Latin being the original text, it is a translation and as far as we can judge, by no means an early translation from the Greek. The idea that its language is closely parallel to Tertullian arises from the fact that Tertullian used the complete Acts of the Passion, and that some African Latin parallelisms can be traced between Tertullian's works and the Latin Acts.

Turning now to the Greek Acts, we find everywhere instead of the word $\lambda\epsilon\acute{o}\pi\alpha\rho\delta os$ (which we should expect if that word were already current, and especially if the redactor of the Acts were acquainted, as Lightfoot affirms, with the Ignatian epistles and under their literary influence) the word $\pi\acute{a}\rho\delta a\lambda\iota s$: and this at once disposes of the argument drawn by Pearson and Lightfoot against Bochart. Perpetua and Felicitas must not be any longer quoted in this argument; or, if quoted, they will be quoted on the other side.

Of course this does not settle the question; many things are still unsettled in the Ignatian controversy: the other instances brought forward by Lightfoot are probably correct; but, in any case, we do not discuss them. Before leaving this point we would, however, draw attention to one remark which Lightfoot makes on the disputed question, which seems to us by some oversight to have fallen a little short of the point which it was meant to establish. In *Ignatius* I. 398 he says, "Where the remains of contemporary literature are so few and fragmentary, intervals far longer than half a century constantly occur between the producible instances of the use of particular words. One example will suffice. The Ignatian letter to the Ephesians on any showing was written before the middle of the third century when it is quoted by Origen. Yet the next example, after this Ignatian letter, of the use of the word ἀναγωγεύς in the same sense as 'a lifting-engine' (Ephes. 9), which the lexicographers produce, is in Eustathius a writer of the twelfth century."

It seems to us that the illustration given fails of its force in that (i) it makes a parallel case between a common word (*leopard*) and a very rare word (ἀναγωγεύς), which itself is being used in a technical sense. Are "lifting-engines" to be expected as frequently in literature as lions and tigers? But (ii), and this is the main point, it is not a question of the occurrence of a rare word, but a question of the occurrence of another very common word as an alternative for the word sought. We have no perplexity on this head with regard to the 'lifting-engine'; but on the other hand where the words 'leopardus' and its Greek form do not occur, there are plenty of pards and panthers and the like occurring as an equivalent description to 'leopard.' It seems therefore that Lightfoot's illustration is not quite adequate.

The second point of relationship between the Acts of Perpetua and Felicitas and the Ignatian Epistles consists in the assumed quotations which the Acts make from the letters.

These quotations are affirmed by Lightfoot, and they consist of one principal instance, and three minor references. The idea is that the Ignatian Epistles and especially the epistle to the Romans became a sort of 'vade-mecum' of martyrs (which is certainly true of many of the current Acta Martyrum), and so naturally coloured the thought and language of Perpetua and her companions.

In *Ignatius* I. 135 we have the references given as follows:

ACTS OF PERPETUA AND FELICITAS (c. A.D. 202).

"The expression 'ut bestias lucraretur' (§ 14) is probably taken from Rom. 5, ὀναίμην τῶν θηρίων κ.τ.λ....These Acts likewise present other coincidences with the Epistles of Ignatius: e.g. § 10, 'Coeperunt me favitores oleo defrigere quomodo solent in agonem' (comp. Ephes. 3, ὑπαλειφθῆναι with the note), and § 18, 'Christi Dei' (comp. Trall. 7, Smyrn. 6, 10, with the note on Ephes. 1, below, II. p. 29 sq.)."

To the above we must add the following from vol. I. p. 335 note. "To the coincidences quoted above from the Acts of Perpetua and Felicitas should be added § 5, 'nos non in nostra potestate esse constitutos sed in Dei'; comp. Polyc. 7, χριστιανὸς ἑαυτοῦ ἐξουσίαν οὐκ ἔχει ἀλλὰ Θεῷ σχολάζει. This document is closely connected with Tertullian (see *de Anim.* 55): and the Ignatian Epistles, if known to the writers of these Acts, were likely to be known to this father also. Thus the parallels in the one tend to confirm the inference drawn from the parallels in the other."

Now with regard to these assumed quotations and references; the first, as will be seen from our Greek text, arises from a misunderstanding; 'ut bestias lucraretur' is a false translation for κερδάνας τὸ μὴ θηριομαχῆσαι, and the martyr is not described in terms that are in any degree parallel to the Ignatian language; he simply has as his reward (in the fact of his dying in prison) that he was exempted from the conflict in the amphitheatre.

The third reference 'Christi Dei' arises from an error in the punctuation of the Latin text which should have a comma after 'Christi' so as to read 'ut matrona Christi, Dei dilecta'; some texts emphasize the punctuation by inserting a second 'ut' between 'Christi' and 'Dei.' It appears then that the two expressions are in apposition and the second is an explanation of the first. But it is more than an explanation, for a reference to the Greek shews that it is a mere gloss of the Latin translator. There is nothing in the Greek text to answer to 'Dei dilecta.'

The fourth instance quoted seems also to be a misunderstanding: the Greek text is, γνῶθι γὰρ ὅτι οὐκ ἐν τῇ ἡμετέρᾳ ἐξουσίᾳ ἀλλ' ἐν τῇ τοῦ Θεοῦ ἐσόμεθα, which must mean that *when the day of trial comes*, 'we shall be at God's disposal and not at our own.' Now this can hardly be deduced from the general proposition in the letter to Polycarp that 'a Christian is not at his own disposal but *devotes his time*' (so Lightfoot translates σχολάζει) 'to God.'

There remains, then, only the second of the instances given by Lightfoot, where he compares Act. Perpet. 10 with Ephes. 3. The figure, however, is such a common one (that of being oiled by one's trainer)[1], and the reading of the passage in the Ignatian

---

[1] The figure is found in Tertullian, *ad Martyras*, c. iii. which tract is closely connected with the time of Perpetua's imprisonment. But when Tertullian speaks of the good fight, in which the living God is the president, and the trainer the Holy Spirit, whose unction the martyrs have received, he is not quoting the Ignatian

letter is so doubtful withal, that I fancy this coincidence will hardly be pressed when it is seen how completely the appearance of the preceding parallelisms is changed by the introduction of the Greek text.

When Lightfoot's great work was first under the notice of the reviewers his use of the Acts of Perpetua was severely commented upon, if we remember rightly, by Hilgenfeld. The critic's objection was, we believe, widely sympathised with. We have now better means of determining whether it was well-founded or not. And in any case it can do no harm to draw attention to the point again.

As we have said above, our remarks are only meant as corrections to the great argument; they are not intended as a challenge to battle. If we honour and admire Dr Lightfoot's scholarship, we have also the good sense to fear him more than anything short of 'thunder and the sword of Michael.' And if we prize his personal kindness, we also remember that on the road by which our studies have in recent years taken us, we passed the 'slovenly unhandsome corse' of the author of *Supernatural Religion*[1].

Authorities for the text.

The Greek text is taken from a MS. in the library of the Convent of the Holy Sepulchre (Cod. S. Sep. 1). The MS. contains βίοι καὶ μαρτυρίαι for the month of February. It is labelled with the name of Symeon Metaphrastes, but inasmuch as the writing is of the tenth century at least the title must not be taken literally. Amongst the interesting matters in this Codex will be found on p. 136 the martyrdom of Polycarp (i.e. the letter of the Smyrneans). On pp. 144—173 the life of Porphyry of Gaza. On p. 173 Hippolytus, *De Christo et Antichristo*. The martyrdom of Perpetua will be found on p. 41 of the MS.

---

epistles. Indeed it is more likely than any other hypothesis that the Perpetua Acts are under the influence of this special tract of Tertullian. As we have said the figure is very ancient, one of the best cases of it is Ps.-Josephus, *De Maccabeis* § 18.

[1] These remarks were written and the substance of the argument communicated to the Society of Biblical Literature and Exegesis, before we had received the news of the immeasurable loss which the Christian world had sustained in the translation of Dr Lightfoot. There are others besides the bishops and clergy who stood around his grave in Auckland Chapel who can use the words "our dear father departed," and who can look back over the work that he did for the defence of learning and of religion, and say as Perpetua said, and without her touch of pity or of scorn, οὐχὶ σὺ πάπας ἡμέτερος εἶ;

The longer Latin version was discovered by Holstein in the monastery of Monte Cassino and published (? after his death), with his notes, by Valesius at Paris. This edition forms the basis of Ruinart's text in the *Acta Martyrum Sincera*. Ruinart used two other MSS.: one from the monastery of Salzburg, the other from the abbey of Compiègne. According to Aubé, the MS. 17626 (fonds latin) in the National Library at Paris belongs to the same group. We have not been able to do more with the Latin text than reprint Ruinart's authorities and correct some of the more evident errors of the Latin transcribers.

PASSIO S. PERPETVAE.

I. Si[1] vetera fidei exempla, et Dei gratiam testificantia et edificationem hominis operantia, propterea in litteris sunt digesta, ut lectione eorum quasi repraesentatione rerum et Deus honoretur et homo confortetur; cur non et nova documenta aeque utrique causae convenientia et digerantur? Vel quia et haec vetera futura quandoque sunt et necessaria posteris, si in praesenti suo tempore minori deputantur auctoritati, propter praesumptam venerationem antiquitatis. Sed viderint qui unam virtutem Spiritus huius Sancti pro aetatibus iudicent temporum; cum maiora reputanda sint novitiora quaeque ut novissimiora, secundum exuberationem gratiae in ultima saeculi spatia decretam[2]. In novissimis enim diebus, dicit Dominus, effundam de Spiritu meo super omnem carnem, et prophetabunt filii filiaeque eorum, et super servos et ancillas meas de meo Spiritu effundam: et iuvenes visiones videbunt, et senes somnia somniabunt. Itaque et nos qui sicut prophetias, ita visiones novas pariter repromissas et agnoscimus et honoramus ceterasque virtutes Spiritus Sancti ad instrumentum Ecclesiae deputamus, cui et missus est, idem omnia donativa administrans in omnibus, prout unicuique distribuit Dominus, necessario et digerimus, et ad gloriam Dei lectione

---

[1] In the following notes H = Holstenius: S = cod. Salisburgensis: C = cod. Compendiensis.
[2] Codd. Ed. *decreta*.

PREF. Two prefatory notes are given in the Greek; one of which is the introduction of the Metaphrast, and the other of the prae-Metaphrast. εὐλόγησον is the proper ejaculation of the ἀναγνώστης.

C. I. Cf. the introduction to the Passion of Cyprian (Ruinart p. 179) where our Acts seem to be alluded to. "Certe durum erat, ut cum majores nostri, *plebeiis* et *catechumenis* martyrium consecutis tantum honoris pro martyrii ipsius veneratione

ΜΑΡΤΥΡΙΟΝ ΠΕΡΠΕΤΟΥΑC.

[Μαρτύριον τῆς ἁγίας Περπετούας καὶ τῶν σὺν αὐτῇ τελειωθέντων ἐν Ἀφρικῇ. τῇ πρὸ τεσσάρων νόνων Φευρουαρίων. Εὐλόγησον.]

[Ἐπὶ Οὐαλεριάνου καὶ Γαληνοῦ διωγμὸς ἐγένετο ἐν ᾧ ἐμαρτύρησαν οἱ ἅγιοι Σάτυρος, Σατουρνῖνος, Ῥευκᾶτος, Περπετούα, Φηλικητάτη, νόναις Φευρουαρίαις.]

I. Εἰ τὰ παλαιὰ τῆς πίστεως δόγματα, καὶ δόξαν Θεοῦ φανεροῦντα καὶ οἰκοδομὴν ἀνθρώποις ἀποτελοῦντα, διὰ τοῦτό ἐστι γεγραμμένα, ἵνα τῇ ἀναγνώσει αὐτῶν ὡς παρουσίᾳ τῶν πραγμάτων χρώμεθα καὶ ὁ θεὸς δοξασθῇ, διατί μὴ καὶ τὰ καινὰ παραδείγματα, ἄτε δὴ ἑκάτερα ἐργαζόμενα ὠφέλειαν, ὡσαύτως 5 γραφῇ παραδοθῇ; ἢ γὰρ τὰ νῦν πραχθέντα οὐ τὴν αὐτὴν παρρησίαν ἔχει, ἐπεὶ δοκεῖ πως εἶναι τὰ ἀρχαῖα σεμνότερα; πλὴν καὶ ταῦτα ὕστερόν ποτε γενόμενα παλαιά, ὡσαύτως τοῖς μεθ' ἡμᾶς γενήσεται καὶ ἀναγκαῖα καὶ τίμια. ἀλλ' ὄψωνται οἵτινες μίαν δύναμιν ἑνὸς ἁγίου πνεύματος κατὰ τὰς ἡλικίας 10 κρίνουσι τῶν χρόνων, ὅτι δὴ δυνατώτερα ἔδει νοῆσθαι τὰ καινότερα, ὡς ἔχοντα αὐξανομένης τῆς χάριτος τῆς εἰς τὰ τέλη
ii. 17. τῶν καιρῶν ἐπηγγελμένης· ἐν ἐσχάταις γὰρ ἡμέραις, λέγει ὁ Κύριος, ἐγχεῶ ἀπὸ τοῦ πνεύματός μου ἐπὶ πᾶσαν σάρκα, καὶ προφητεύσουσιν οἱ υἱοὶ ὑμῶν καὶ αἱ θυγατέρες ὑμῶν· καὶ οἱ 15 νεανίσκοι ὑμῶν ὁράσεις ὄψονται, καὶ οἱ πρεσβῦται ὑμῶν ἐνυπνίοις ἐνυπνισθήσονται. ἡμεῖς δὲ οἵτινες προφητείας καὶ ὁράσεις καινὰς δεχόμεθα καὶ ἐπιγινώσκομεν καὶ τιμῶμεν πάσας τὰς δυνάμεις τοῦ ἁγίου πνεύματος, ὡς χορηγεῖ τῇ ἁγίᾳ ἐκκλησίᾳ πρὸς ἣν καὶ ἐπέμφθη, πάντα τὰ χαρίσματα ἐν πᾶσιν διοικοῦν, 20 ἑκάστῳ ὡς ἐμέρισεν ὁ θεός, ἀναγκαίως καὶ ἀναμιμνήσκομεν καὶ πρὸς οἰκοδομὴν εἰσάγομεν, μετὰ ἀγάπης ταῦτα ποιοῦντες εἰς

Praefatio. Γαλινοῦ. Σατουρνίλος.   C. 1, l. 1. εἶτα.   2. φανερουνται.
6. παραδοθείς.   11. ὅτε δὲ.   13. επηγγειλμενης.   14. εκχεω.

dederint, ut de passionibus eorum multa, aut prope dixerim cuncta conscripserint, ut ad nostram quoque notitiam *qui nondum nati fuimus* pervenerint, Cypriani tanti sacerdotis et tanti martyris praeteriretur."

celebramus, ut ne qua aut imbecillitas, aut desperatio fidei apud veteres tantum aestimet gratiam divinitatis conversatam, sive martyrum, sive in revelationum dignatione: cum semper Deus operetur quae repromisit, non credentibus in testimonium, credentibus in beneficium. Et nos itaque quod audivimus et contrectavimus annuntiamus et vobis, fratres et filioli, ut et vos qui interfuistis, rememoremini gloriae Domini: et qui nunc cognoscitis per auditum, communionem habeatis cum sanctis martyribus, et per illos cum Domino Jesu Christo, cui est claritas et honor in saecula saeculorum. Amen.

II. Apprehensi sunt adolescentes catechumini, Revocatus et Felicitas conserva eius, Saturninus[1] et Secundulus. Inter quos et Vibia[2] Perpetua, honeste nata, liberaliter instituta, matronaliter nupta, habens patrem et matrem et fratres duos; alterum aeque catechuminum, et filium infantem ad ubera. Erat autem ipsa annorum circiter viginti duorum. Haec ordinem totum martyrii sui iam huic ipsa narrabit, sicut conscriptum manu sua et suo sensu reliquit.

III. Cum adhuc, inquit, cum persecutoribus essemus[3], et me pater avertere[4], et deicere pro sua affectione perseveraret: Pater,

---

[1] In H deest *Saturninus*.
[2] H habet *Inter hos Ubia Perpetua, honesta, liberaliter educata, matrona licet nupta*.   [3] H, *essem*.   [4] H, *evertere cupiret*.

C. II. Of the names given in the Acts, all can be paralleled from the African inscriptions.

Perhaps the best illustration can be taken from the inscriptions at Zanfur.

C. I. L. VIII. 1803   FELICITAS.
                       P. V. A.
                       H. S. E.
        1808   D. M. S
                       Q. MAGNIVS
                       SATVRNINVS
                       P.V. AN. CV.
        1817   D. M. S
                       REVOCATVS
                       V.A. XXV.

For the use of the term σύνδουλοι cf. the Numidian inscription 2296.

                       DIS MA S
                       FLORVS T FLAVI
                       T F MINIANI CI
                       SER. PIVS VIXIT
                       . FORTVNATA
                       CONSERVA
                       PIO MARITO
                       MVNVMEN
                       TVM FEC

ΜΑΡΤΥΡΙΟΝ ΠΕΡΠΕΤΟΥΑC.

δόξαν Θεοῦ καὶ ἵνα μή πως ᾖ ἀβέβαιός τις καὶ ὀλιγόπιστος, ἢ καὶ τοῖς παλαιοῖς μόνον τὴν χάριν καὶ τὴν δύναμιν δίδοσθαι νομίσῃ, εἴτε ἐν τοῖς τῶν μαρτύρων εἴτε ἐν τοῖς τῶν ἀποκαλύψεων ἀξιώμασιν· πάντοτε ἐργαζομένου τοῦ θεοῦ ἃ ἐπηγγείλατο εἰς μαρτύριον μὲν τῶν ἀπίστων εἰς ἀντίληψιν δὲ τῶν πιστῶν.

Καὶ ἡμεῖς ἃ ἠκούσαμεν καὶ ἑωράκαμεν καὶ ἐψηλαφήσαμεν εὐαγγελιζόμεθα ὑμῖν, ἀδελφοὶ καὶ τέκνα, ἵνα καὶ οἱ συμπαρόντες ἀναμνησθῶσιν δόξης Θεοῦ καὶ οἱ νῦν δι' ἀκοῆς γινώσκοντες κοινωνίαν ἔχητε μετὰ τῶν ἁγίων μαρτύρων καὶ δι' αὐτῶν μετὰ τοῦ Κυρίου ἡμῶν Ἰησοῦ Χριστοῦ, ᾧ ἡ δόξα εἰς τοὺς αἰῶνας τῶν αἰώνων. ἀμήν.

II. Ἐν πόλει Θουβουρβιτάνων τῇ μικροτέρᾳ συνελήφθησαν νεανίσκοι κατηχούμενοι, Ῥεουκᾶτος καὶ Φηλικητάτη, σύνδουλοι, καὶ Σατουρνῖνος, καὶ Σεκοῦνδος· μετ' αὐτῶν δὲ καὶ Οὐιβία Περπετούα ἥτις ἦν γεννηθεῖσα εὐγενῶς καὶ τραφεῖσα πολυτελῶς γαμηθεῖσά τε ἐξόχως. Αὕτη εἶχεν πατέρα καὶ μητέρα καὶ δύο ἀδελφοὺς ὧν ὁ ἕτερος ἦν ὡσαύτως κατηχούμενος· εἶχεν δὲ καὶ τέκνον ὃ πρὸς τοῖς μασθοῖς ἔτι ἐθήλαζεν· ἦν δὲ αὕτη ἐτῶν εἴκοσι δύο· ἥτις πᾶσαν τὴν τάξιν τοῦ μαρτυρίου ἐντεῦθεν διηγήσατο, ὡς καὶ τῷ νοΐ αὐτῆς καὶ τῇ χειρὶ συγγράψασα κατέλιπεν οὕτως εἰποῦσα.

III. Ἔτι, φησίν, ἡμῶν παρατηρουμένων ἐπεχείρει ὁ πατήρ μοι λόγοις πείθειν με κατὰ τὴν ἑαυτοῦ εὐσπλαγχνίαν τῆς προκειμένης ὁμολογίας ἐκπεσεῖν· κἀγὼ πρὸς αὐτόν· Πάτερ,

---

1. ἡ ἀβεβαιόστης.   5. cod. εις αντιεις αντιληψιν.   C. II., l. 13. θουκριτανων.
14. φηληκητατη.   15. Σατορνιλος.   15. Ἰουλια και Περπετουα.
17. αὕτη.   19. αὕτη.   24. ευσπλαχνιαν.

I quote this inscription because it furnishes us with the suggestion that perhaps Revocatus may have been the husband of Felicitas; and also because it contains the name Minianus which is very like the perplexing Timinianus whom we find later on in the story.

For the name Felicitas as a slave's name see C. I. L. VIII. 1897.

```
        D. M. S
       FELICITAS
     V. A. iii. H.S.E
      HILARVS AVGGG
     LIB. VERNACVLAE
        SVAE FEC.
```

inquio, vides, verbi gratia, vas hoc iacens, urceolum, sive aliud? Et dixit: Video, et ego dixi ei: Numquid alio nomine vocari potest, quam quod est? Et ait: Non. Sic et ego aliud me dicere non possum, nisi quod sum, Christiana. Tunc pater motus in hoc verbo, misit se in me ut oculos mihi erueret: sed vexavit tantum, et profectus[1] est victus cum argumentis diaboli. Tunc paucis diebus quod caruissem patre, Domino gratias egi, et refrigerata[2] sum absentia illius. In ipso spatio paucorum dierum baptizati sumus: mihi autem Spiritus dictavit, nihil aliud petendum ab[3] aqua, nisi sufferentiam carnis. Post paucos dies recipimur in carcerem, et expavi quia numquam experta eram tales tenebras. O diem asperum! Aestus validos[4] turbarum beneficio, concussurae militum! Novissime macerabar sollicitudine infantis. Ibi tunc Tertius et Pomponius benedicti Diacones qui nobis ministrabant, constituerunt pretio, ut paucis horis emissi in meliorem locum carceris refrigeraremus. Tunc exeuntes de carcere universi sibi vacabant. Ego infantem lactabam jam inedia defectum. Sollicita pro eo adloquebar matrem, et confortabam[5] fratrem commendabam filium. Tabescebam ideo quod illos tabescere videram mei beneficio. Tales sollicitudines multis diebus passa sum, et usurpavi ut mecum infans in carcere maneret; et statim convalui et relevata sum a labore et sollicitudine infantis: et factus est mihi carcer subito quasi praetorium, ut ibi mallem esse quam alibi[6].

IV. Tunc dixit mihi frater meus: Domina soror, iam in magna dignitate[7] es, tanta ut postules visionem, et ostendatur tibi, an passio sit, an commeatus. Et ego quae me sciebam fabulari cum Domino, cuius beneficia[8] tanta experta eram, fidenter repromisi[9] ei dicens: Crastina die tibi renuntiabo. Et postulavi, et ostensum est mihi hoc. Video scalam aeream[10] mirae magni-

---

[1] H, profecto.   [2] H, refrigeravit.
[3] Ed., in; H, ab.   [4] H, validus.
[5] S, et confortabam, fratri commendabam filium.   [6] H, alicubi.
[7] H, in magna dignatione es, tanta ut postulem.   [8] S, beneficio.
[9] S, repromissionibus ejus dixi.   [10] Ed. and C, auream. S, aeream.

C. IV. This ladder appears again, rather unskilfully imitated in the Martyrdom of S. Sadoth and his companions in Persia (Ruinart, *Acta Sincera* p. 504): "Vidi in somniis hac nocte scalam cum magna gloria, cuius initium erat in caelo. Ei autem superstabat sanctus episcopus cum infinita gloria, ego vero infra in

ἔφην, ὁρᾷς λόγου χάριν σκεῦος κείμενον ἢ ἄλλο τι τῶν τοιούτων; κἀκεῖνος ἀπεκρίθη· Ὁρῶ· κἀγώ· Ἄλλο ὀνομάζειν αὐτὸ μὴ θέμις; οὐδὲ δύναμαι, εἰ μὴ ὃ εἰμί, τουτέστι Χριστιανή.

Τότε ὁ πατήρ μου ταραχθεὶς τῷδε τῷ λόγῳ ἐπελθὼν ἠθέλησεν τοὺς ὀφθαλμούς μου ἐξορύξαι· ἔπειτα μόνον κράξας, ἐξῆλθεν νικηθεὶς μετὰ τῶν τοῦ διαβόλου μηχανῶν.

Τότε ὀλίγας ἡμέρας ἀποδημήσαντος αὐτοῦ, ηὐχαρίστησα τῷ Κυρίῳ καὶ ἥσθην ἀπόντος αὐτοῦ· καὶ ἐν αὐταῖς ταῖς ἡμέραις ἐβαπτίσθημεν· καὶ ἐμὲ ὑπηγόρευσεν τὸ πνεῦμα τὸ ἅγιον μηδὲν ἄλλο αἰτήσασθαι ἀπὸ τοῦ ὕδατος τοῦ βαπτίσματος εἰ μὴ σαρκὸς ὑπομονήν. μετὰ δὲ ὀλίγας ἡμέρας ἐβλήθημεν εἰς φυλακὴν καὶ ἐξενίσθην· οὐ γὰρ πώποτε τοιοῦτον ἑωράκειν σκότος, ὡς δεινὴν ἡμέραν καῦμά τε σφοδρόν, καὶ γὰρ ἀνθρώπων πλῆθος ἦν ἐκεῖ ἄλλως τε καὶ στρατιωτῶν συκοφαντίαις πλείσταις· μεθ' ἃ δὴ πάντα κατεπονούμην διὰ τὸ νήπιον τέκνον. τότε Τέρτιος καὶ Πομπόνιος, εὐλογημένοι διάκονοι οἱ διηκόνουν ἡμῖν, τιμὰς δόντες ἐποίησαν ἡμᾶς εἰς ἡμερώτερον τόπον τῆς φυλακῆς μεταχθῆναι. τότε ἀναπνοῆς ἐτύχομεν, καὶ δὴ ἕκαστοι προσαχθέντες ἐσχόλαζον ἑαυτοῖς· καὶ τὸ βρέφος ἠνέχθη πρός με, καὶ ἐπεδίδουν αὐτῷ γάλα, ἤδη αὐχμῷ μαρανθέν· τῇ μητρὶ προσελάλουν, τὸν ἀδελφὸν προετρεπόμην, τὸ νήπιον παρετιθέμην· ἐτηκόμην δὲ ὅτι ἐθεώρουν αὐτοὺς δι' ἐμὲ λυπουμένους· οὕτως περίλυπος πλείσταις ἡμέραις οὖσα, εἴθισα καὶ τὸ βρέφος ἐν τῇ φυλακῇ μετ' ἐμοῦ μένειν· κἀκεῖνο ἀνέλαβεν καὶ ἐγὼ ἐκουφίσθην ἀπὸ ἀνίας καὶ πόνου, καὶ ἰδοὺ ἡ φυλακὴ ἐμοὶ γέγονεν πραιτώριον, ὡς μᾶλλόν με ἐκεῖ θέλειν εἶναι, καὶ οὐκ ἀλλαχοῦ.

IV. Τότε εἶπέν μοι ὁ ἀδελφός Κυρία ἀδελφή, ἤδη ἐν μεγάλῳ ἀξιώματι ὑπάρχεις τοσαύτη οὖσα ὡς εἰ αἰτήσειας ὀπτασίας, ὀπτασίαν λάβοις ἂν εἰς τὸ δειχθῆναί σοι εἴπερ ἀναβολὴν ἔχεις ἢ παθεῖν μέλλεις. κἀγὼ ἥτις ᾔδειν με ὁμιλοῦσαν Θεῷ, οὗ γε δὴ τοσαύτας εὐεργεσίας εἶχον, πίστεως πλήρης οὖσα, ἐπηγγειλάμην αὐτῷ εἰποῦσα· Αὔριόν σοι ἀπαγγελῶ. ᾐτησάμην δέ, καὶ ἐδείχθη μοι τοῦτο·

C. III., l. 1. κείμενον: forsitan addendum est ἢ ὀστράκινον.   6. μόνον.
12. ἐκλήθημεν.   15. πλησται.   17. Παμπονιος.   24. ηθησα.
C. IV., l. 29. αιτησας.   31. ητις: cod. αιτεις.

---

terra consistebam. Atque ille magna me cum hilaritate compellans, Ascende, inquit."

tudinis pertingentem usque ad caelum, et ita angustam, per quam nonnisi singuli ascendere possent: et in lateribus scalae omne genus ferramentorum infixum. Erant ibi gladii, lanceae, hami, macherae, ut si quis negligenter, aut non sursum adtendens ascenderet, laniaretur et carnes ejus inhaererent ferramentis. Et erat sub ipsa scala draco cubans mirae magnitudinis, qui ascendentibus insidias parabat[1], et exterrebat ne ascenderent. Ascendit autem Saturus prior, qui postea se propter nos ultro tradiderat, et tunc cum apprehensi sumus praesens non fuerat: et pervenit in caput scalae, et convertit se[2] et dixit mihi: Perpetua, sustineo te. Sed vide ne te mordeat draco ille. Et dixi ego: Non me nocebit in nomine Domini Jesu Christi. Et desub ipsa scala quasi timens me, lente[3] elevavit caput: et cum primum gradum calcassem, calcavi illius caput. Et ascendi, et vidi spatium horti immensum, et in medio horti sedentem hominem canum, in habitu pastoris, grandem, oves mulgentem: et circumstantes candidatos millia multa. Et levavit caput et adspexit me, et dixit mihi: Bene venisti, tegnon. Et clamavit me, et de caseo quod mulgebat dedit mihi quasi buccellam, et ego accepi iunctis manibus, et manducavi: et universi circumstantes dixerunt, Amen. Et ad sonum vocis experrecta sum, commanducans adhuc dulcis nescio quid. Et retuli statim fratri meo, et intelleximus passionem esse futuram. Et coepimus nullam iam spem in saeculo habere.

V. Post paucos dies rumor cucurrit ut audiremur. Supervenit autem et de civitate pater meus, consumptus taedio, ascendit ad me ut me deiceret, dicens: Miserere, filia, canis meis; miserere patri, si dignus sum a te pater vocari. Si his te manibus ad hunc

---

[1] H, praestabat.　　　　[2] Ed. addit *ad me*, quod in H deest.
[3] H, lente ejecit caput, et quasi primum.

Ἀμήν. The 'Amen' shews that she is describing the reception of the Eucharist. This is also evident from the joined or crossed hands with which the fragment was received. Even in S. Paul's time the Eucharistic Amen was a prominent feature of the Service: the unlearned or private persons joined in it ("else how could the unlearned say the Amen at thy Thanksgiving," 1 Cor. xiv. 16). The utterance of this Amen is commonly spoken of by the Fathers as a shout, and here also the whole company join in it so that we need not be surprised that at this point Perpetua waked. If it appears strange that this Amen should in the vision follow the participation in the elements, instead of forming a part of the consecration, we have only to remember that the same thing occurs in the Teaching of the Apostles ("after ye are filled, give thanks as follows"). The rapidity of the action from the reception of the elements to the close of the ritual is a characteristic of the world of visions. On account of their use of bread and

Εἶδον κλίμακα χαλκῆν θαυμαστοῦ μήκους· ἧς τὸ μῆκος ἄχρις οὐρανοῦ· στενὴ δὲ ἦν ὡς μηδένα δι' αὐτῆς δύνασθαι εἰ μὴ μοναχὸν ἕνα ἀναβῆναι· ἐξ ἑκατέρων δὲ τῶν τῆς κλίμακος μερῶν πᾶν εἶδος ἦν ἐμπεπηγμένον ἐκεῖ ξιφῶν δοράτων ἀγκίστρων μαχαιρῶν ὀβελίσκων· ἵνα πᾶς ὁ ἀναβαίνων ἀμελῶς καὶ μὴ ἀναβλέπων τοῖς ἀκοντίοις τὰς σάρκας σπαραχθείη· ἦν δὲ ὑπ' αὐτῇ τῇ κλίμακι δράκων ὑπερμεγέθης, ὃς δὴ τοὺς ἀναβαίνοντας ἐνήδρευεν ἐκθαμβῶν ὅπως μὴ τολμῶσιν ἀναβαίνειν· ἀνέβη δὲ ὁ Σάτυρος· ὃς δὴ ὕστερον δι' ἡμᾶς ἑκὼν παρέδωκεν ἑαυτόν· αὐτοῦ γὰρ καὶ οἰκοδομὴ ἦμεν· ἀλλ' ὅτε συνελήφθημεν ἀπῆν· ὡς οὖν πρὸς τὸ ἄκρον τῆς κλίμακος παρεγένετο, ἐστράφη, καὶ εἶπεν· Περπετούα, περιμένω σε· ἀλλὰ βλέπε μή σε ὁ δράκων δάκῃ· καὶ εἶπον· Οὐ μή με βλάψῃ, ἐν ὀνόματι Ἰησοῦ Χριστοῦ. Καὶ ὑποκάτω τῆς κλίμακος ὡσεὶ φοβούμενός με ἠρέμα τὴν κεφαλὴν προσήνεγκεν· καὶ ὡς εἰς τὸν πρῶτον βαθμὸν ἠθέλησα ἐπιβῆναι τὴν κεφαλὴν αὐτοῦ ἐπάτησα· [καὶ ἀνέβην] καὶ εἶδον ἐκεῖ κῆπον μέγιστον καὶ ἐν μέσῳ τοῦ κήπου ἄνθρωπον πολιὸν καθεζόμενον ποιμένος σχῆμα ἔχοντα ὑπερμεγέθη ὃς ἤλμευγε τὰ πρόβατα· περιειστήκεισαν δὲ αὐτῷ πολλαὶ χιλιάδες λευχειμονούντων· ἐπάρας δὲ τὴν κεφαλὴν ἐθεάσατό με καὶ εἶπεν· Καλῶς ἐλήλυθας, τέκνον· καὶ ἐκάλεσέν με, καὶ ἐκ τοῦ τυροῦ οὗ ἤλμευγεν ἔδωκέν μοι ὡσεὶ ψωμίον· καὶ ἔλαβον ζεύξασα τὰς χεῖράς μου καὶ ἔφαγον· καὶ εἶπαν πάντες οἱ παρεστῶτες Ἀμήν.

Καὶ πρὸς τὸν ἦχον τῆς φωνῆς ἐξυπνίσθην ἔτι τί ποτε μασωμένη γλυκύ· καὶ εὐθέως διηγησάμην τῷ ἀδελφῷ καὶ ἐνοήσαμεν ὅτι δέοι παθεῖν· καὶ ἠρξάμην ἔκτοτε μηδεμίαν ἐλπίδα ἐν τῷ αἰῶνι τούτῳ ἔχειν.

V. Μετὰ δὲ ἡμέρας ὀλίγας ἔγνωμεν μέλλειν ἡμᾶς ἀκουσθήσεσθαι· παρεγένετο δὲ καὶ ὁ πατὴρ ἐκ τῆς πολλῆς ἀποδημίας μαραινόμενος καὶ ἀνέβη πρός με προτρεπόμενός με καταβαλεῖν, λέγων· Θύγατερ, ἐλέησον τὰς πολιάς μου, ἐλέησον τὸν πατέρα σου, εἴπερ ἄξιός εἰμι ὀνομασθῆναι πατήρ σου, μνήσθητι ὅτι ταῖς

1. κλῆμα καχαλκην. 3. κληματος. 4. αγχιστρων. 13. deest εν.
16. deest καὶ ἀνέβην (cf. Lat. et ascendi). 19. λευσχημονονουντων.
26. εννοησαμεν.

---

cheese in the Eucharist, the Montanists obtained the nickname of Ἀρτοτυρῖται. See Epiph. *Haer.* 49. 2. The explanation which was given of this curious custom in later times refers it to an assimilation of the Eucharistic oblation to the offerings of primitive man, viz.: the fruits of field and flock; but this is very doubtful; and it is probable that the true explanation is historical rather than theological.

florem aetatis provexi; si te praeposui omnibus fratribus tuis, ne me dederis in dedecus hominum. Aspice ad fratres tuos, aspice ad matrem tuam et materteram, aspice ad filium tuum qui post te vivere non poterit. Depone animos. Ne[1] universos nos extermines: nemo enim nostrum libere loquetur, si tu aliquid fueris passa. Haec dicebat pater pro sua pietate basians mihi manus; et se ad pedes meos iactans, et lacrymis non filiam, sed dominam me vocabat. Et ego dolebam causam[2] patris mei, quod solus de passione mea gavisurus non esset de toto genere meo; et confortavi eum, dicens: Hoc fiet in illa catasta quod Deus voluerit. Scito enim nos non in nostra potestate esse constitutos, sed in Dei. Et recessit a me contristatus.

VI. Alio die cum pranderemus, subito rapti sumus ut audiremur, et pervenimus ad forum. Rumor statim per vicinas fori partes cucurrit, et factus est populus immensus. Ascendimus in catastam[3]. Interrogati ceteri confessi sunt. Ventum est et ad me. Et apparuit pater illico cum filio meo, et extraxit me de gradu, et dixit supplicans: Miserere infanti[4]. Et Hilarianus[5] Procurator, qui tunc loco proconsulis Minuci Timiniani defuncti ius gladii acceperat: Parce, inquit, canis patris tui, parce infantiae pueri. Fac sacrum pro salute Imperatorum. Et ego respondi: Non facio. Hilarianus, Christiana es? inquit. Et ego respondi: Christiana sum. Et cum staret pater ad me deiciendam, iussus est ab Hilariano deici, et virga percussus est. Et doluit mihi casus patris mei, quasi ego fuissem percussa: sic dolui pro senecta

[1] S and C, et noli nos universos exterminare.
[2] Ed. canos. H, causam.
[3] Ed., in catasta. S, catastam. C, in catastam.
[4] C and S habent *canos meos* pro *infanti*.
[5] S semper habet *Elarianus*, C Helarianus.

C. v. "Catasta" seems to be the regular African term for the platform in front of the judge, or as we should say, the bar. Cf. Augustin. in Ps. 137 (de martyre Crispina), "Gaudebat Crispina cum ligata producebatur, cum in catasta levabatur, cum audiebatur, cum damnabatur."

τοὺς θυμούς. This seems to be rendered 'presumptio' in the Acta Montani.

C. VI. A similar case of the delegation of Proconsular powers will be found in the Acta S. Montani (Ruinart p. 201): "et continuo eadem die subito rapti sumus ad Procuratorem qui defuncti Proconsulis partes administrabat." The evidence of this particular document is however vitiated by the suspicion that the author imitates the Acts of Perpetua.

τῶν δορυφόρων τις ἐτύπτησεν. Cf. Ps.-Josephus De Maccab. 6, λάξ γέ τοι τῶν

ΜΑΡΤΥΡΙΟΝ ΠΕΡΠΕΤΟΥΑC. 47

χερσὶν ταύταις πρὸς τὸ τοιοῦτον ἄνθος τῆς ἡλικίας ἀνήγαγόν σε· καὶ προειλόμην σε ὑπὲρ τοὺς ἀδελφούς σου· [ὅρα τοὺς ἀδελφούς σου,] ὅρα τὴν σὴν μητέρα καὶ τὴν τῆς μητρός σου ἀδελφήν, ἴδε τὸν υἱόν σου ὃς μετὰ σὲ ζῆν οὐ δύναται· ἀπόθου τοὺς θυμοὺς καὶ μὴ ἡμᾶς πάντας ἐξολοθρεύσῃς· οὐδεὶς γὰρ 5 ἡμῶν μετὰ παρρησίας λαλήσει ἐάν τί σοι συμβῇ.

Ταῦτα ἔλεγεν ὡς πατὴρ κατὰ τὴν τῶν γονέων εὔνοιαν· καὶ κατεφίλει μου τὰς χεῖρας καὶ ἑαυτὸν ἔρριπτεν ἔμπροσθεν τῶν ποδῶν μου καὶ ἐπιδακρύων οὐκέτι με θυγατέρα ἀλλὰ κυρίαν ἐπεκάλει· ἐγὼ δὲ περὶ τῆς διαθέσεως τοῦ πατρὸς ἤλγουν, ὅτι ἐν 10 ὅλῳ τῷ ἐμῷ γένει μόνος οὐκ ἠγαλλιᾶτο ἐν τῷ ἐμῷ πάθει. παρεμυθησάμην δὲ αὐτὸν εἰποῦσα· Τοῦτο γενήσεται ἐν τῷ βήματι ἐκείνῳ ἐὰν θέλῃ ὁ κύριος· γνῶθι γὰρ ὅτι οὐκ ἐν τῇ ἡμετέρᾳ ἐξουσίᾳ, ἀλλ' ἐν τῇ τοῦ θεοῦ ἐσόμεθα· καὶ ἐχωρίσθη ἀπ' ἐμοῦ ἀδημονῶν.
15

VI. Καὶ τῇ ἡμέρᾳ ἐν ᾗ ὥριστο ἡρπάγημεν ἵνα ἀκουσθῶμεν· καὶ ὥσπερ ἐγενήθημεν εἰς τὴν ἀγοράν, φήμη εὐθὺς εἰς τὰ ἐγγὺς μέρη διῆλθεν καὶ συνέδραμεν πλεῖστος ὄχλος· ὡς δὲ ἀνέβημεν εἰς τὸ βῆμα ἐξετασθέντες οἱ λοιποὶ ὡμολόγησαν· ἤμελλον δὲ κἀγὼ ἐξετάζεσθαι· καὶ ἐφάνη ἐκεῖ μετὰ τοῦ τέκνου μου ὁ πατήρ· 20 καὶ καταγαγών με πρὸς ἑαυτόν, εἶπεν· Ἐπίθυσον ἐλεήσασα τὸ βρέφος. καὶ Ἱλαριάνος ἐπίτροπος, ὃς τότε τοῦ ἀνθυπάτου ἀποθανόντος Μινουκίου Ὀππιάνου ἐξουσίαν εἰλήφει μαχαίρας, λέγει μοι· Φεῖσαι τῶν πολιῶν τοῦ πατρός σου· φεῖσαι τῆς τοῦ παιδίου νηπιότητος· ἐπίθυσον ὑπὲρ σωτηρίας τῶν αὐτοκρατόρων. 25 κἀγὼ ἀπεκρίθην· Οὐ θύω. καὶ εἶπεν Ἱλαριάνος· Χριστιανὴ εἶ; καὶ εἶπον· Χριστιανή εἰμι. καὶ ὡς ἐσπούδαζεν ὁ πατήρ μου καταβαλεῖν [ἀπὸ τῆς ὁμολογίας], κελεύσαντος Ἱλαριάνου ἐξεβλήθη· προσέτι δὲ καὶ τῇ ῥάβδῳ τῶν δορυφόρων τις ἐτύπτησεν αὐτόν· κἀγὼ σφόδρα ἤλγησα, ἐλεήσασα τὸ γῆρας αὐτοῦ· τότε 30

2. omisit cod. ὅρα τους ἀδελφούς σου per ὁμοιοτέλευτον. Cf. Lat.   C. vi.
l. 16. Interpres latinus legit ἐν ᾧ ἤριστων.   18. πληστος.   22. Ἰλαριανοστις.   23. Οπιανου.   26. ηλαριανος.   28. απο της ομυλογιας: forsitan additamentum.

πικρῶν τις δορυφόρων εἰς τοὺς κενεῶνας ἐναλλόμενος ἔτυπτεν, and 17, ἔλεγον δὲ καὶ τῶν δορυφόρων τινές. It is certain that almost all the early Christian martyrologies are under the influence of the Maccabee legends. Several of the apocryphal martyrdoms such as the Passion of S. Symphorosa and the story of Felicitas and her seven sons are direct imitations of these Jewish martyrdoms. In other cases their

eius misera. Tunc nos universos pronuntiat, et damnat ad bestias, et hilares descendimus ad carcerem. Tunc quia consueverat a me infans mammas accipere, et mecum in carcere manere; statim mitto ad patrem Pomponium[1] diaconum, postulans infantem: sed pater dare noluit, et quomodo Deus voluit, neque ille amplius mammas desideravit; neque mihi fervorem fecerunt: ne sollicitudine infantis et dolore mammarum macerarer.

VII. Post dies paucos, dum universi oramus, subito media oratione profecta est mihi vox, et nominavi Dinocratem: et obstupui quod numquam mihi in mentem venisset nisi tunc, et dolui commemorata casus eius. Et cognovi me statim dignam esse, et pro eo petere[2] debere. Et coepi pro ipso orationem facere multum, et ingemiscere ad Dominum. Continuo ipsa nocte ostensum est mihi hoc in oramate: Video Dinocratem exeuntem de loco tenebroso, ubi et complures[3] erant, aestuantem et sitientem valde, sordido vultu, et colore pallido, et vulnus in facie eius quod cum moreretur habuit. Hic Dinocrates fuerat frater meus carnalis, annorum septem, qui per infirmitatem facie cancerata[4] male obiit, ita ut mors eius odio fuerit omnibus hominibus. Pro hoc ego orationem feceram: et inter me et illum grande erat diastema[5] ita ut uterque ad invicem accedere non possemus. Erat deinde in ipso loco ubi Dinocrates erat, piscina plena aqua, altiorem marginem habens quam erat statura pueri, et extendebat se Dinocrates quasi bibiturus. Ego dolebam quod et piscina illa aquam habebat, et tamen propter altitudinem marginis bibiturus non esset. Et experrecta sum, et cognovi fratrem meum laborare. Sed confidebam[6] me profuturam labori eius, et orabam pro eo omnibus diebus quousque transivimus in carcerem castrensem. Munere enim castrensi eramus pugnaturi. Natale tunc Getae Caesaris,

---

[1] C, Pompinianum.
[2] S, pati.
[3] H, complura erant loca tenebrosa.
[4] S, macerata.
[5] Sic suspicatur Holsten. S, dianten. Ed., diadema.
[6] S, considerabam. H, fidebam me profuturam labori.

---

influence is no less marked, as in the case of the Acts of SS. Jacobus, Marianus &c., (Ruinart, *Acta Sinc.* p. 199), "his peractis *Maccabaico gaudio* Mariani mater exultans &c." and in the Acts of SS. Montanus, Lucius etc. (Ruinart p. 205), "O Maccabaicam matrem &c." We are inclined then to believe that the language of our Acts is coloured here by reminiscence of the Acts of the Maccabees. It is true that the father of Perpetua does not make an exact parallel with the aged Eleazar, for he is not a Christian; but the preceding sentences in the Acts have a further

ΜΑΡΤΥΡΙΟΝ ΠΕΡΠΕΤΟΥΑϹ.

ἡμᾶς πάντας πρὸς θηρία κατακρίνει· καὶ χαίροντες κατήμεν εἰς φυλακήν.

Ἐπειδὴ δὲ ὑπ' ἐμοῦ ἐθηλάζετο τὸ παιδίον, καὶ μετ' ἐμοῦ ἐν τῇ φυλακῇ εἰώθει μένειν, πέμπω πρὸς τὸν πατέρα μου Πομπόνιον διάκονον, αἰτοῦσα τὸ βρέφος· ὁ δὲ πατὴρ οὐκ ἔδωκεν· πλὴν ὡς ὁ θεὸς ᾠκονόμησεν οὔτε ὁ παῖς μασθοὺς ἐπεθύμησεν ἔκτοτε, οὔτε ἐμοί τις προσγέγονεν φλεγμονή· ἴσως ἵνα [μὴ] καὶ τῇ τοῦ παιδίου φροντίδι καὶ τῇ τῶν μασθῶν ἀλγηδόνι καταπονηθῶ.

VII. Καὶ μετ' ὀλίγας ἡμέρας προσευχομένων ἡμῶν ἁπάντων ἐξαίφνης ἐν μέσῳ τῆς προσευχῆς ἀφῆκα φωνὴν καὶ ὠνόμασα Δεινοκράτην. καὶ ἔκθαμβος ἐγενήθην, διότι οὐδέποτε εἰ μὴ τότε ἀνάμνησιν αὐτοῦ πεποιήκειν· ἤλγησα δὲ εἰς μνήμην ἐλθοῦσα τῆς αὐτοῦ τελευτῆς. πλὴν εὐθέως ἔγνων ἐμαυτὴν ἀξίαν οὖσαν αἴτησιν ποιήσασθαι περὶ αὐτοῦ, καὶ ἠρξάμην πρὸς Κύριον μετὰ στεναγμῶν προσεύχεσθαι τὰ πλεῖστα· καὶ εὐθέως αὐτῇ τῇ νυκτὶ ἐδηλώθη μοι τοῦτο. ὁρῶ Δεινοκράτην ἐξερχόμενον ἐκ τόπου σκοτεινοῦ, ὅπου καὶ ἄλλοι πολλοὶ καυματιζόμενοι καὶ διψῶντες ἦσαν, ἐσθῆτα ἔχοντα ῥυπαράν· ὠχρὸν τῇ χρόᾳ· καὶ τὸ τραῦμα ἐν τῇ ὄψει αὐτοῦ περιὸν ἔτι, ὅπερ τελευτῶν εἶχεν· (οὗτος δὲ ὁ Δεινοκράτης, ὁ ἀδελφός μου κατὰ σάρκα, ἑπταετὴς τεθνήκει ἀσθενήσας καὶ τὴν ὄψιν αὐτοῦ γαγγραίνῃ σαπεὶς ὡς τὸν θάνατον αὐτοῦ στυγητὸν γενέσθαι πᾶσιν ἀνθρώποις·) ἐθεώρουν οὖν μέγα διάστημα ἀνὰ μέσον αὐτοῦ καὶ ἐμοῦ, ὡς μὴ δύνασθαι ἡμᾶς ἀλλήλοις προσελθεῖν. ἐν ἐκείνῳ δὲ τῷ τόπῳ ἐν ᾧ ἦν ὁ ἀδελφός μου κολυμβήθρα ἦν ὕδατος πλήρης· ὑψηλωτέραν δὲ εἶχεν τὴν κρηπῖδα ὑπὲρ τὸ τοῦ παιδίου μῆκος· πρὸς ταύτην ὁ Δεινοκράτης διετείνετο πιεῖν προαιρούμενος· ἐγὼ δὲ ἤλγουν διότι καὶ ἡ κολυμβήθρα ἦν πλήρης ὕδατος, καὶ τὸ παιδίον οὐκ ἠδύνατο πιεῖν διὰ τὴν ὑψηλότητα τῆς κρηπῖδος· καὶ ἐξυπνίσθην.

Καὶ ἔγνων κάμνειν τὸν ἀδελφόν μου· ἐπεποίθειν δὲ δύνασθαί με αὐτῷ βοηθῆσαι ἐν ταῖς ἀνὰ μέσον ἡμέραις, ἐν αἷς κατήχθημεν εἰς τὴν ἄλλην φυλακὴν τὴν τοῦ χιλιάρχου· ἐγγὺς γὰρ ἦν τῆς παρεμβολῆς οὗ ἠμέλλομεν θηριομαχεῖν· γενέθλιον γὰρ

---

6. Cod. ουται.   7. μὴ deest in cod.   C. vii., l. 19. Cod. τελευτων, οπερ περιων ετι ειχεν.   20. ος αδελφος.

---

analogy with the Jewish legend, since πείσθητι ταῖς τοῦ βασιλέως ἐντολαῖς in one text is not unlike in idea to the ἐπίθυσον ὑπὲρ σωτηρίας τῶν αὐτοκρατόρων.

et feci pro illo orationem die et nocte gemens et lacrymans ut mihi donaretur.

VIII. Die autem quo in nervo mansimus, ostensum est mihi hoc. Video locum illum quem retro videram tenebrosum, esse lucidum; et Dinocratem mundo corpore, bene vestitum, refrigerantem, et ubi erat vulnus, video cicatricem; et piscinam illam quam retro videram, summisso margine usque ad umbilicum pueri; et aquam de ea trahebat sine cessatione, et super margine phiala erat aurea[1] plena aqua; et accessit Dinocrates, et de ea bibere coepit, quae phiala non deficiebat. Et satiatus abscessit de aqua ludere more infantium gaudens, et experrecta sum. Tunc intellexi translatum eum esse de poena.

IX. Deinde post dies paucos Pudens[2], miles Optio, praepositus carceris, qui nos[3] magni facere coepit intelligens magnam virtutem Dei esse in nobis, multos fratres ad nos admittebat, ut et nos et illi invicem refrigeraremus. Ut autem proximavit dies muneris, intravit ad me pater meus consumtus taedio, et coepit barbam suam evellere, et se in terram mittere, et prosternere se in faciem, et improperare annis suis, et dicere tanta verba, quae moverent universam creaturam. Ego dolebam pro infelici senecta eius.

X. Pridie quam pugnaremus, video in oramate huc venisse Pomponium diaconum ad ostium carceris, et pulsare vehementer; exivi ad eum, et aperui ei: qui erat vestitus distinctam candidam, habens multiplices caligulas[4]. Et dixit mihi: Perpetua te ex-

---

[1] Sic H. In Ed. deest.   [2] S, Prudens.
[3] H, qui nos magnifaciebat; capit intelligere magnam virtutem esse in nobis, qui multos ad nos.   [4] S, galliculas. Ed., calliculas.

C. VIII. ἐν νέρβῳ. We need not be surprised at the Latinism which can be paralleled from similar writings to our own. It is interesting to note that Tertullian in his tract *ad Martyras* written about this time to a band of martyrs in prison at Carthage sympathises with them over their suffering in the stocks; but remarks that if the mind be in Heaven, the leg will not really suffer upon earth.

φιάλη μεστή. Cf. *Passio Cypriani* 197, "tunc ibi Cyprianus phialam quae super marginem fontis iacebat, arripuit: et cum illam de fontis rivulis implesset, hausit."

C. IX. *Optio.* The earlier commentators seem to have been puzzled over this word as applied to a prison official, though they were able to quote a passage from Ambrose, *Ep. ad Ephes.* c. 4, where *optio carceris* is used. A reference to the African inscriptions will shew that it was a very common word indeed, and just the word to be used either by a writer of Latin Acts or a translator of Greek Acts at this point. It is the general word for any lieutenant of a higher officer. *C. I. L.* VIII. 2482 has no less than four Optiones, all from the same legion and engaged in the same votive offering. This inscription belongs to the time of

ΜΑΡΤΥΡΙΟΝ ΠΕΡΠΕΤΟΥΑC.

ἤμελλεν ἐπιτελεῖσθαι [Γέτα] Καίσαρος. εἶτα προσευξαμένη μετὰ στεναγμῶν σφοδρῶς περὶ τοῦ ἀδελφοῦ μου ἡμέρας τε καὶ νυκτὸς δωρηθῆναί μοι αὐτὸν ἠξίωσα.

VIII. Καὶ εὐθὺς ἐν τῇ ἑσπέρᾳ ἐν ᾗ ἐν νέρβῳ ἐμείναμεν, ἐδείχθη μοι τοῦτο.

Ὁρῶ τὸν τόπον ἐν ᾧ ἑωράκειν τὸν Δεινοκράτην [φωτεινὸν ὄντα, καὶ τὸν Δεινοκράτην] καθαρῷ σώματι ὄντα, καὶ καλῶς ἠμφιεσμένον καὶ ἀναψύχοντα· καὶ ὅπου τὸ τραῦμα ἦν οὐλὴν ὁρῶ· καὶ ἡ κρηπὶς τῆς κολυμβήθρας κατήχθη ἕως τοῦ ὀμφαλίου αὐτοῦ· ἔρρεεν δὲ ἐξ αὐτῆς ἀδιαλείπτως ὕδωρ· καὶ ἐπάνω τῆς κρηπίδος ἦν χρυσῆ φιάλη μεστή· καὶ προσελθὼν ὁ Δεινοκράτης ἤρξατο ἐξ αὐτῆς πίνειν· ἡ δὲ φιάλη οὐκ ἐνέλειπεν· καὶ ἐμπλησθεὶς ἤρξατο παίζειν ἀγαλλιώμενος ὡς τὰ νήπια· καὶ ἐξυπνίσθην.

Καὶ ἐννόησα ὅτι μετετέθη ἐκ τῶν τιμωριῶν.

IX. Καὶ μετ' ὀλίγας ἡμέρας Πούδης τις στρατιώτης ὁ τῆς φυλακῆς προιστάμενος μετὰ πολλῆς σπουδῆς ἤρξατο ἡμᾶς τιμᾶν καὶ δοξάζειν τὸν θεόν, ἐννοῶν δύναμιν μεγάλην εἶναι περὶ ἡμᾶς· διὸ καὶ πολλοὺς εἰσελθεῖν πρὸς ἡμᾶς οὐκ ἐκώλυεν εἰς τὸ ἡμᾶς διὰ τῶν ἐπαλλήλων παραμυθιῶν παρηγορεῖσθαι. ἤγγισεν δὲ ἡ ἡμέρα τῶν φιλοτιμιῶν καὶ εἰσέρχεται πρός με ὁ πατήρ, τῇ ἀκηδίᾳ μαρανθείς, καὶ ἤρξατο τὸν πώγωνα τὸν ἴδιον ἐκτίλλειν, ῥίπτειν τε ἐπὶ γῆς, καὶ πρηνὴς κατακείμενος κακολογεῖν τὰ ἑαυτοῦ ἔτη κατηγορῶν καὶ λέγων τοιαῦτα ῥήματα ὡς πᾶσαν δύνασθαι τὴν κτίσιν σαλεῦσαι· ἐγὼ δὲ ἐπένθουν διὰ τὸ ταλαίπωρον γῆρας αὐτοῦ.

X. Πρὸ μιᾶς οὖν τοῦ θηριομαχεῖν ἡμᾶς, βλέπω ὅραμα τοιοῦτον.

Πομπόνιος ὁ διάκονος, φησίν, ἦλθεν πρὸς τὴν θύραν τῆς φυλακῆς καὶ ἔκρουσεν σφόδρα· ἐξελθοῦσα ἤνοιξα αὐτῷ· καὶ ἦν ἐνδεδυμένος ἐσθῆτα λαμπρὰν καὶ περιεζωσμένος· εἶχεν δὲ ποικίλα ὑποδήματα καὶ λέγει μοι· Σὲ περιμένω, ἐλθέ.

1. Cod. om. Γετα, quia in pref. Valerianum et Gallienum nominavit. C. VIII., l. 6. τον τοπον. Cod. τοπω: cod. om. φωτεινον οντα και τον Δεινοκρατην per ὁμοιοτελευτον. Cf. Lat. 7. καλλως. C. IX., l. 15. πουδης τισρατιωτης (sic). 16. Cod. add. της ante σπουδης.

Valerian and Gallienus. It does not however seem to be a very early military term; indeed Festus says "optio, *qui nunc dicitur*, antea appellabatur adcensus; is adiutor centurioni dabatur a tribuno militum." This agrees with what we find in C. VII., that they had been removed from the common prison εἰς τὴν φυλακὴν τοῦ χιλιάρχου. We may add that in Acts xvi. 23, 27, 36, Codex Bezae has *optio* as the rendering of δεσμοφύλαξ.

C. x. ποικίλα ὑποδήματα. The beautiful shoes appear also in the epitaph of Abercius.

spectamus, veni. Et tenuit mihi manum, et coepimus ire per aspera loca et flexuosa. Vix tandem pervenimus anhelantes ad amphitheatrum, et induxit me in media arena, et dixit mihi: Noli pavere, hic sum tecum, et conlaboro tecum, et abiit. Et adspicio populum ingentem attonitum. Et quia sciebam me ad bestias datam esse, mirabar quod non mitterentur mihi bestiae. Et exivit quidam contra me Aegyptius foedus specie cum adiutoribus suis pugnaturus mecum. Veniunt et ad me adolescentes decori adiutores et favitores mei. Et expoliata sum, et facta sum masculus. Et coeperunt me favitores mei oleo defricare[1], quomodo solent in agonem, et illum contra Aegyptium video in afa[2] volutantem. Et exivit vir quidam mirae magnitudinis, ut etiam excederet fastigium amphitheatri, discinctam[3] habens tunicam et purpuram inter duos clavos per medium pectus, habens et caligulas[4] multiformes ex auro et argento factas, et ferens[5] virgam quasi lanista, et ramum viridem, in quo erant mala aurea. Et petiit silentium, et dixit: Hic Aegyptius si hanc vicerit, occidet illam gladio; et si hunc vicerit accipiet ramum istum. Et recessit. Et accessimus ad invicem, et coepimus mittere pugnos. Ille mihi pedes apprehendere volebat[6], ego autem illi calcibus faciem caedebam. Et sublata sum in aere, et coepi eum sic caedere quasi terram concalcans. At ubi vidi moram fieri, iunxi manus, ita ut digitos in digitos mitterem. Et apprehendi illi caput, et cecidit in faciem; et calcavi illi caput. Et coepit populus clamare, et favitores mei psallere. Et accessi ad lanistam, et accepi ramum. Et osculatus est me, et dixit mihi: Filia pax tecum. Et coepi

---

[1] Sic S, Ed. defrigere.
[2] C and S, aqua.
[3] H, discinctatus purpuram.
[4] S, galliculas.
[5] H, efferens.
[6] Sic, H. Ed. habet *quaerebat*.

εἰς Ῥώμην ὃς ἔπεμψεν ἐμὲν βασίληαν ἀθρῆσαι
καὶ βασίλισσαν ἰδεῖν χρυσόστολον χρυσοπέδιλον.

Lightfoot (*Ign.* I. 482) explains this of the Church, basing it upon Ps. xlv. (liv.) 10 . παρέστη ἡ βασίλισσα ἐκ δεξιῶν σου ἐν ἱματισμῷ διαχρύσῳ περιβεβλημένη, πεποικιλμένη· where we may compare the last word with the ποικίλα of the Acts; and lower down ποικίλα ἐκ χρυσίου καὶ ἀργυρίου. With this interpretation of Lightfoot, Ramsay also agrees. It is likely that more than one passage of Scripture has contributed to this curious idea of the Church in her beautiful slippers; for instance there is Cant. vii. 2 τί ὡραιώθησαν διαβήματά σου ἐν ὑποδήμασιν, θύγατερ Ἀμιναδάβ; or Isaiah lii. 7 might be quoted.

ΜΑΡΤΥΡΙΟΝ ΠΕΡΠΕΤΟΥΑΣ.

Καὶ ἐκράτησεν τὰς χεῖράς μου καὶ ἐπορεύθημεν διὰ τραχέων καὶ σκολιῶν τόπων· καὶ μόλις παρεγενόμεθα εἰς τὸ ἀμφιθέατρον· καὶ εἰσήγαγέν με εἰς τὸ μέσον καὶ λέγει μοι· Μὴ φοβήθῃς· ἐνθάδε εἰμὶ μετὰ σοῦ, συγκάμνων σοι· καὶ ἀπῆλθεν.

Καὶ ἰδοὺ βλέπω πλεῖστον ὄχλον ἀποβλέποντα τῇ θεωρίᾳ σφόδρα· κἀγὼ ἥτις εἶδον πρὸς θηρία με καταδικασθεῖσαν ἐθαύμαζον ὅτι οὐκ ἔβαλλόν μοι αὐτά.

Καὶ ἦλθεν πρός με Αἰγύπτιός τις ἄμορφος τῷ σχήματι μετὰ τῶν ὑπουργούντων αὐτῷ μαχησόμενός μοι· καὶ ἔρχεται πρός με νεανίας τις εὐμορφώτατος τῷ κάλλει ἐξαστράπτων, καὶ ἕτεροι μετ᾽ αὐτοῦ νεανίαι ὡραῖοι· ὑπηρέται τε σπουδασταὶ ἐμοί. καὶ ἐξεδύθην καὶ ἐγενήθην ἄρρην· καὶ ἤρξαντο οἱ ἀντιλήπτορές μου ἐλαίῳ με ἀλείφειν, ὡς ἔθος ἐστὶν ἐν ἀγῶνι· καὶ ἄντικρυς βλέπω τὸν Αἰγύπτιον ἐκεῖνον ἐν τῷ κονιορτῷ κυλιόμενον.

Ἐξῆλθεν δέ τις ἀνὴρ θαυμαστοῦ μεγέθους, ὑπερέχων τοῦ ἄκρου τοῦ ἀμφιθεάτρου, διεζωσμένος ἐσθῆτα ἥτις εἶχεν οὐ μόνον ἐκ τῶν δύο ὤμων τὴν πορφύραν, ἀλλὰ καὶ ἀνὰ μέσον ἐπὶ τοῦ στήθους· εἶχεν δὲ καὶ ὑποδήματα ποικίλα ἐκ χρυσίου καὶ ἀργυρίου· ἐβάσταζεν δὲ καὶ ῥάβδον ὡς βραβευτὴς ἢ προστάτης μονομάχων· ἔφερεν δὲ καὶ κλάδους χλωροὺς ἔχοντας μῆλα χρυσᾶ· καὶ αἰτήσας σιγὴν γενέσθαι, ἔφη· Οὗτος ὁ Αἰγύπτιος ἐὰν ταύτην νικήσῃ ἀνελεῖ αὐτὴν μαχαίρᾳ· αὕτη δὲ ἐὰν νικήσῃ αὐτὸν λήψεται τὸν κλάδον τοῦτον· καὶ ἀπέστη. προσήλθομεν δὲ ἀλλήλοις καὶ ἠρξάμεθα παγκρατιάζειν· ἐκεῖνος ἐμοῦ τοὺς πόδας κρατεῖν ἠβούλετο· ἐγὼ δὲ λακτίσμασιν τὴν ὄψιν αὐτοῦ ἔτυπτον· καὶ ἰδοὺ *ἐπῆρα ἀπὸ ἀέρος* καὶ ἠρξάμην αὐτὸν οὕτω τύπτειν ὡς μὴ πατοῦσα τὴν γῆν.

Ἰδοῦσα δὲ ὡς οὐδέπω ἤκιζον αὐτὸν ζεύξασα τὰς χεῖράς μου καὶ δακτύλους δακτύλοις ἐμβαλοῦσα τῆς κεφαλῆς αὐτοῦ ἐπελαβόμην· καὶ ἔρριψα αὐτὸν ἐπ᾽ ὄψει καὶ ἐπάτησα τὴν κεφαλὴν αὐτοῦ· καὶ ἤρξατο πᾶς ὁ ὄχλος βοᾶν· καὶ οἱ σπουδασταί μου ἐγαυρίων· καὶ προσῆλθον τῷ βραβευτῇ καὶ ἔλαβον τὸν κλάδον· καὶ ἠσπάσατό με καὶ εἶπεν· Εἰρήνη μετὰ σοῦ, θύγατερ· καὶ

1. τραχεων. C. x., l. 4. συγκαμνον σου. 5. πιστὸν. 6. καγω cod. και. 12. αντιλημπτορες. 14. κοιλιομενον. 16. διεξοσμενος. 19. προστατων. 23. λειψεται. 26. forsitan επηρα αεριος.

Is this thought of the shoes the reason why Saturus says in c. xii. πόδας δὲ αὐτοῦ οὐκ ἐθεασάμεθα?

54   PASSIO S. PERPETVAE.

ire cum gloria ad portam Sanavivariam. Et experrecta sum: et intellexi me non ad bestias, sed contra diabolum esse pugnaturam; sed sciebam mihi victoriam imminere[1]. Hoc usque in pridie muneris egi: ipsius autem muneris actum, si quis voluerit, scribat.

XI. Sed et Saturus benedictus hanc visionem suam edidit, quam ipse conscripsit. Passi, inquit, eramus, et exivimus de carne, et coepimus ferri a quatuor Angelis in Orientem, quorum manus nos non tangebant. Ibamus autem non supini sursum versi, sed quasi mollem clivum[2] ascendentes. Et liberati primum[3] iam mundo vidimus lucem immensam; et dixi: Perpetua (erat enim haec in latere meo), hoc est quod nobis Dominus promittebat: percepimus promissionem. Et dum gestamur ab ipsis quatuor Angelis, factum est nobis spatium grande, quod tale fuit quasi viridarium, arbores habens rosae[4], et omne genus floris. Altitudo autem arborum erat in modum cypressi, quarum folia cadebant[5] sine cessatione. Ibi autem in viridario, alii quatuor Angeli fuerunt clariores ceteris, qui ubi viderunt nos, honorem[6] nobis dederunt, et dixerunt ceteris Angelis: Ecce[7] sunt, ecce sunt: cum admiratione. Et expavescentes quatuor illi Angeli qui gestabant nos, deposuerunt nos: et pedibus nostris transivimus stadium via[8] lata. Ibi invenimus Iocundum et Saturninum[9] et Artaxium, qui eandem persecutionem passi vivi arserunt; et

[1] H, esse.   [2] C, glebam.
[3] Ed., primam iam vidimus. H, primo mundo vidimus. C, primum iam mundo vidimus.
[4] S, rosam.   [5] S, ardebant.   [6] S, et honorem.
[7] S and C, ecce sunt. Expavescentes cum admiratione quatuor illi Angeli qui stabant deposuerunt nos.
[8] H, violata.   [9] In S and C deest Saturninum.

C. XI. κυπάρισσον. Cf. *Passio Cypriani* p. 197, "iter autem nobis erat per locum prati amoenum et viridantium nemorum laeta fronde vestitum opacum cupressis consurgentibus in excelsum et pinnis pulsantibus caelum."

Ἦσαν δὲ μεθ' ἡμῶν κτέ.

The Latin text may be taken as more correct here, although at first sight the introduction of four new angels has little meaning. It is probable that these are the four Angels of the Presence (the Face-angels, cf. Is. lxiii. 9, who, by a natural misunderstanding, appear as four faces in the book of Enoch, where they are given as Michael, Rufael, Gabriel and Fanuel, *Enoch* c. 40). As to their being more glorious than the others, this is not a casual remark; we may compare it with 2 Pet. ii. 11 ὅπου ἄγγελοι ἰσχύι καὶ δυνάμει μείζονες ὄντες κτέ. This passage is the equivalent of Jude 9 where only one superior angel is spoken of (ὁ ἀρχάγγελος), viz. Michael. It thus appears that 2 Peter has substituted the Face-angels for

ΜΑΡΤΥΡΙΟΝ ΠΕΡΠΕΤΟΥΑC. 55

ἠρξαμεν εὐθὺς πορεύεσθαι μετὰ δόξης πρὸς πύλην τὴν λεγομένην ζωτικήν· καὶ ἐξυπνίσθην.

Καὶ ἐννόησα ὅτι οὐ πρὸς θηρία μοι ἀλλὰ πρὸς τὸν διάβολόν ἐστιν ἡ ἐσομένη μάχη· καὶ συνῆκα ὅτι νικήσω αὐτόν.

Ταῦτα ἕως πρὸ μιᾶς τῶν φιλοτιμιῶν ἔγραψα· τὰ ἐν τῷ ἀμφιθεάτρῳ γενησόμενα ὁ θέλων συγγραψάτω.

XI. Ἀλλὰ καὶ ὁ μακάριος Σάτυρος τὴν ἰδίαν ὀπτασίαν αὐτὸς δι' ἑαυτοῦ συγγράψας ἐφανέρωσεν τοιαῦτα εἰρηκώς.

Ἤδη, φησίν, ἦμεν ὡς πεπυνθότες καὶ ἐκ τῆς σαρκὸς ἐξεληλύθειμεν, καὶ ἠρξάμεθα βαστάζεσθαι ὑπὸ τεσσάρων ἀγγέλων πρὸς ἀνατολάς, καὶ αἱ χεῖρες [αὐτῶν] ἡμῶν οὐχ ἥπτοντο· ἐπορευόμεθα δὲ εἰς τὰ ἀνώτερα, καὶ οὐχ ὕπτιοι ἀλλ' οἷον ὡς δι' ὁμαλῆς ἀναβάσεως ἐφερόμεθα.

Καὶ δὴ ἐξελθόντες τὸν πρῶτον κόσμον φῶς λαμπρότατον εἴδομεν· καὶ εἶπον πρὸς τὴν Περπετούαν (πλησίον γάρ μου ἦν), τοῦτό ἐστιν ὅπερ ὁ Κύριος ἡμῶν ἐπηγγείλατο· μετειλήφαμεν τῆς ἐπαγγελίας· αἰωρουμένων δὲ ἡμῶν διὰ τῶν τεσσάρων ἀγγέλων ἐγένετο στάδιον μέγα, ὅπερ ὡσεὶ κῆπος ἦν, ἔχον ῥόδου δένδρα καὶ πᾶν γένος τῶν ἀνθέων· τὸ δὲ ὕψος τῶν δένδρων ἦν ὡσεὶ κυπαρίσσου μῆκος, ἀκαταπαύστως δὲ κατεφέρετο τὰ δένδρα τὰ φύλλα αὐτῶν.

Ἦσαν δὲ μεθ' ἡμῶν ἐν αὐτῷ τῷ κήπῳ οἱ τέσσαρες ἄγγελοι, ἀλλήλων ἐνδοξότεροι, ὑφ' ὧν ἐφερόμεθα· πτοουμένους δὲ ἡμᾶς καὶ θαυμάζοντας [καὶ] ἀπέθηκαν, καὶ *ἀναλαβόντες τὴν ὁδὸν διήλθομεν τὸ στάδιον τοῖς ἡμετέροις ποσίν.

Ἐκεῖ εὕρομεν Ἰουκοῦνδον καὶ Σάτυρον, καὶ Ἀρτάξιον τοὺς ἐν αὐτῷ τῷ διωγμῷ ζῶντας κρεμασθέντας· εἴδομεν δὲ Κοΐντον

---

1. ἠρξωμεν.   3. ενοησα.   4. εσωμενη.   C. XI., l. 9. εξεληλυθημεν.   11. αυτων deest.   ουχιπτοντο (sic).   17. εωρουμενων.   18. εχων.
20. κηπαρησου (sic).   ακαταπαστως.   24. cod. και απεθηκαν και ανελαβον και οδον λαβοντες.

Michael, under the general term "the angels that are superior in strength and might." Appropriately then our Acts speak of the four great angels as excelling in glory.

ζῶντας κρεμασθέντας. At first sight it seems as if the Greek were here giving us something equivalent to *vivum cremari* as is not uncommon in writers who are of bilingual habit. Certainly the word ζῶντας would lead us to expect some such words as κατακαυθέντας, for burning alive was a common form of martyrdom. Cf. *Mart. Polyc.* c. v. fin.: *Mart. Petri Andreae &c.* (Ruinart p. 135) "tu igitur sacrifica ne turpiter te illusam vivam incendam." *Acta Tryphonis* (p. 138) "tales iussit imperator vivos incendi nisi sacrificaverint diis" etc. On the other hand observe

Quintum, qui et ipse martyr in carcere exierat; et quaerebamus de[1] illis ubi essent ceteri. Dixerunt autem nobis Angeli: Venite prius, introite, et salutate Dominum.

XII. Et venimus prope locum, cuius loci parietes tales erant, quasi de luce aedificati; et ante ostium loci illius quatuor Angeli stabant, qui introeuntes vestierunt stolas candidas. Et nos vestiti introivimus, et vidimus lucem immensam, et audivimus[2] vocem unitam dicentium: Agios, agios, agios; sine cessatione. Et vidimus in medio loci illius sedentem quasi hominem canum, niveos habentem capillos, et vultu iuvenili, cuius pedes non vidimus. Et in dextra, et in sinistra seniores[3] quatuor et post illos ceteri seniores complures stabant: et introeuntes cum admiratione, stetimus ante thronum; et quatuor Angeli sublevaverunt nos: et osculati sumus illum, et de manu sua traiecit nobis in faciem[4]. Et ceteri seniores dixerunt nobis: Stemus. Et stetimus, et pacem fecimus. Et dixerunt nobis seniores: Ite, et ludite. Et dixi: Perpetua, habes quod vis. Et dixit mihi: Deo gratias, ut quomodo in carne hilaris fui, hilarior sum et hic modo.

XIII. Et exivimus, et vidimus ante fores Optatum episcopum ad dexteram, et Aspasium presbyterum doctorem ad sinistram, separatos et tristes, et miserunt se ad pedes nobis, et dixerunt nobis: Componite inter nos quia existis et sic nos relinquitis. Et diximus illis: Non[5] tu es Papa noster, et tu Presbyter, ut[6] quid vos ad pedes nostros mittatis? Et moti sumus et complexi illos sumus. Et coepit Perpetua graece[7] cum illis loqui, et segregavimus eos in viridarium[8] sub arbore rosae. Et dum loquimur cum eis, dixerunt illis Angeli: Sinite illos, refrigerent[9]; et si quas

---

[1] Sic H and C. S and Ed. habent ab.   [2] H, et introivimus et audivimus.

[3] Seniores......stetimus. Sic H, Ed. autem habet seniores viginti quatuor, et post illos ceteri complures stabant. Introivimus cum magna admiratione et stetimus.

[4] Sic H, Ed. facie.   [5] S, nonne.

[6] H, ut vos ad pedes nobis mittatis. Et moti sumus. Ed. habet *misimus nos* pro *moti sumus*.

[7] Sic S and C. In Ed. deest *graece*.

[8] Sic H, Ed. viridario.   [9] S and C, quiescite et refrigerate.

---

that there are at least two methods of hanging, one by the neck when life becomes almost immediately extinct: and one by the arms or by impalement; the latter requires the word 'living' to explain it fully. In the Martyrdoms of Lyons and Vienne Blandina was hanged in this way on a kind of cross, ἐπὶ ξύλου κρεμασθεῖσα προὔκειτο βορὰ τῶν προσβαλλομένων θηρίων.

τὸν μάρτυρα τὸν ἐν τῇ φυλακῇ ἀποθανόντα· ἐζητοῦμεν δὲ καὶ περὶ τῶν λοιπῶν ποῦ ἄρα εἰσίν· καὶ εἶπον οἱ ἄγγελοι πρὸς ἡμᾶς· Δεῦτε πρῶτον ἔσω ἵνα ἀσπάσησθε τὸν Κύριον.

XII. Καὶ ἤλθομεν πλησίον τοῦ τόπου ἐκείνου τοῦ ἔχοντος τοίχους ὡσανεὶ ἐκ φωτὸς ᾠκοδομημένους, καὶ πρὸ τῆς θύρας τοῦ τόπου ἐκείνου εἰσελθόντες οἱ τέσσαρες ἄγγελοι ἐνέδυσαν ἡμᾶς λευκὰς στολάς· καὶ εἰσήλθομεν καὶ ἠκούσαμεν φωνὴν ἡνωμένην λεγόντων· Ἅγιος, ἅγιος, ἅγιος, ἀκαταπαύστως. καὶ εἴδομεν ἐν μέσῳ τοῦ τόπου ἐκείνου καθεζόμενον ὡς ἄνθρωπον πολιόν· οὗ αἱ τρίχες ὅμοιαι χιόνος καὶ νεαρὸν τὸ πρόσωπον αὐτοῦ· πόδας δὲ αὐτοῦ οὐκ ἐθεασάμεθα. πρεσβύτεροι δὲ τέσσαρες ἐκ δεξιῶν καὶ τέσσαρες ἐξ εὐωνύμων ἦσαν αὐτοῦ· ὀπίσω δὲ τῶν τεσσάρων πολλοὶ πρεσβύτεροι.

Ὡς δὲ θαυμάζοντες εἰσεληλύθαμεν καὶ ἔστημεν ἐνώπιον τοῦ θρόνου, οἱ τέσσαρες ἄγγελοι ἐπῆραν ἡμᾶς, καὶ ἐφιλήσαμεν αὐτόν, καὶ τῇ χειρὶ περιέλαβεν τὰς ὄψεις ἡμῶν· οἱ δὲ λοιποὶ πρεσβύτεροι εἶπον πρὸς ἡμᾶς, Σταθῶμεν καὶ προσευξώμεθα. καὶ εἰρηνοποιήσαντες ἀπεστάλημεν ὑπὸ τῶν πρεσβυτέρων, λεγόντων, Πορεύεσθε καὶ χαίρεσθε.

Καὶ εἶπον, Περπετούα, ἔχεις ὃ ἐβούλου. καὶ εἶπεν, Τῷ θεῷ χάρις ἵνα, ὡς ἐν σαρκὶ μετὰ χαρᾶς ἐγενόμην, πλείονα χαρῶ νῦν.

XIII. Ἐξήλθομεν δὲ καὶ εἴδομεν πρὸ τῶν θυρῶν Ὀπτάτον τὸν ἐπίσκοπον καὶ Ἀσπάσιον τὸν πρεσβύτερον πρὸς τὰ ἀριστερὰ μέρη διακεχωρισμένους καὶ περιλύπους. καὶ πεσόντες πρὸς τοὺς πόδας ἡμῶν ἔφασαν ἡμῖν· Διαλλάξατε ἡμᾶς πρὸς ἀλλήλους ὅτι ἐξεληλύθατε καὶ οὕτως ἡμᾶς ἀφήκατε. καὶ εἴπαμεν πρὸς αὐτούς, Οὐχὶ σὺ πάπας ἡμέτερος εἶ, καὶ σὺ πρεσβύτερος; ἵνα τί οὕτω προσεπέσατε τοῖς ἡμετέροις ποσίν; καὶ σπλαγχνισθέντες περιελάβομεν αὐτοὺς καὶ ἤρξατο ἡ Περπετούα Ἑλληνιστὶ μετ' αὐτῶν ὁμιλεῖν, καὶ ἀνεχωρήσαμεν σὺν αὐτοῖς εἰς τὸν κῆπον ὑπὸ τὸ δένδρον τοῦ ῥόδου. καὶ λαλούντων αὐτῶν μεθ' ἡμῶν ἀπεκρίθησαν οἱ ἄγγελοι πρὸς αὐτούς· Ἐάσατε αὐτοὺς ἀναψύξαι, καὶ εἴ τινας διχοστασίας

C. xii. Cf. *Ep. ad Diognet.* xi. 4, οὗτος ὁ ἀπ' ἀρχῆς, ὁ καινὸς φανεὶς καὶ παλαιὸς εὑρεθείς.

C. xiii. Cf. Hermas, *Vis.* iii. 1. 9, ὁ εἰς τὰ δεξιὰ μέρη τόπος ἄλλων ἐστίν, τῶν ἤδη εὐαρεστηκότων τῷ θεῷ καὶ παθόντων εἵνεκα τοῦ ὀνόματος.

The Latin translator, not understanding the force of the allusion to the left-hand, adds words of explanation: Optatus was on the right-hand and Aspasius on the left.

habetis inter vos dissensiones, dimittite vobis invicem. Et conturbaverunt eos. Et dixerunt Optato: Corrige plebem tuam; quia sic ad te conveniunt quasi de circo redeuntes, et de factionibus[1] certantes. Et sic nobis visum est quasi vellent claudere portas. Et coepimus illic multos fratres cognoscere[2], sed et martyres. Universi odore inenarrabili alebamur, qui nos satiabat. Tunc gaudens experrectus sum.

XIV. Hae visiones insigniores ipsorum martyrum beatissimorum Saturi et Perpetuae, quas ipsi conscripserunt. Secundulum vero Deus maturiore exitu de saeculo, adhuc in carcere evocavit, non sine gratia, ut bestias lucraretur. Gladium[3] tamen etsi non anima, certe caro eius agnovit.

XV. Circa Felicitatem vero, (nam et illi gratia Domini eiusmodi contigit) cum octo iam mensium suum ventrem haberet, (nam praegnans fuerat apprehensa:) instante spectaculi die, in magno erat luctu[4], ne propter ventrem differretur; quia non licet praegnantes poenae repraesentari: et ne inter alios[5] postea sceleratus, sanctum et innocentem sanguinem funderet. Sed et commartyres eius graviter contristabantur, ne tam bonam sociam, quasi comitem, solam in via eiusdem spei relinquerent. Coniuncto itaque unito gemitu, ad Dominum orationem fuderunt ante tertium diem muneris. Statim post orationem dolores eam

---

[1] H, de fatigationibus.   [2] C, cognoscere Martyres, ubi odore.
[3] Sic H, Ed. gaudium.   [4] S, luctae.   [5] Sic H, Ed. aliquos.

ἀλλά γε καὶ τοὺς μάρτυρας. This is the passage referred to by Tertullian in *de Anima* 55, "Quomodo Perpetua fortissima martyr, sub die passionis, in revelatione paradisi, solos illic commartyres suos vidit, nisi quia nullis romphaea paradisi janitrix cedit, nisi quia in Christo decesserint, non in Adam?" From this passage we have inferred that Tertullian knew the Acts in their complete form, i.e. Perpetua's vision + Saturus', since he cites as a vision of Perpetua what is really a part of the vision of Saturus. The reasoning is not wholly convincing, because in the vision of Saturus, Perpetua is imagined to be present, and to see what he sees. We observe that Tertullian here brings forward the undoubtedly Montanistic belief that Paradise is reserved for those who have suffered for the Name. Upon which Cardinal Orsi remarks, in the desire to repel the allegation of Montanism from the martyrs; "sed aut fallitur aperte Tertullianus aut fallit: solos enim se in Paradiso vidisse martyres Perpetua non dicit: quin oppositum clare et aperte testatur: 'et coepimus illic multos fratres cognoscere sed et martyres.' Igitur non solos ibi commartyres sed et confratres etiam eosque non paucos Perpetua seu potius Saturus vidit." There is some force in Cardinal Orsi's objection; nevertheless it is pretty certain that the passage especially in the Greek does contain an emphasis on the martyrs; the usage of ἀλλά γε καί seems to be late and not to differ

ἔχετε μεθ' ἑαυτῶν, ἄφετε ὑμεῖς ἀλλήλοις· καὶ ἐπέπληξαν αὐτοὺς καὶ εἶπαν Ὀπτάτῳ· Ἐπανόρθωσαι τὸ πλῆθός σου, οὕτω γὰρ συνέρχονται πρός σε, ὡσεὶ ἀπὸ ἱπποδρομιῶν ἐπανερχόμενοι καὶ περὶ αὐτῶν φιλονεικοῦντες. ἐνομίζομεν δὲ αὐτοὺς ὡς θέλειν ἀποκλεῖσαι τὰς πύλας. καὶ ἠρξάμεθα ἐκεῖ πολλοὺς τῶν ἀδελφῶν ἐπιγινώσκειν, ἀλλάγε καὶ τοὺς μάρτυρας· ἐτρεφόμεθα δὲ πάντες ὀσμῇ ἀνεκδιηγήτῳ ἥτις οὐκ ἐχόρταζεν ἡμᾶς· καὶ εὐθέως χαίρων ἐξυπνίσθην.

XIV. Αὗται αἱ ὁράσεις ἐμφανέσταται τῶν μαρτύρων Σατύρου καὶ Περπετούας ἃς αὐτοὶ συνεγράψαντο· τὸν γὰρ Σεκοῦνδον τάχειον ἐκ τοῦ κόσμου μετεπέμψατο [ὁ θεός]· ἐν γὰρ τῇ φυλακῇ τῆς κλήσεως ἠξιώθη σὺν τῇ χάριτι πάντως κερδάνας τὸ μὴ θηριομαχῆσαι· πλὴν εἰ καὶ μὴ τὴν σάρκα ἀλλοῦνγε τὴν ψυχὴν αὐτοῦ διεξῆλθεν τὸ ξίφος.

XV. Ἀλλὰ καὶ τῇ Φηλικητάτῃ ἡ χάρις τοῦ θεοῦ τοιαύτη ἐδόθη. ἐκείνη γὰρ συλληφθεῖσα ὀκτὼ μηνῶν ἔχουσα γαστέρα, παννωδύρετο (διότι οὐκ ἔξεστιν ἐγκύμονα θηριομαχεῖν ἢ τιμωρεῖσθαι), μήπως ὕστερον μετὰ ἄλλων ἀνοσίων ἐκχυθῇ τὸ αἷμα αὐτῆς τὸ ἀθῷον.

Ἀλλὰ καὶ οἱ συμμάρτυρες αὐτῆς περίλυποι ἦσαν σφόδρα οὕτω καλὴν συνεργὸν καὶ ὡσεὶ συνοδοιπόρον ἐν ὁδῷ τῆς αὐτῆς ἐλπίδος μὴ θέλοντες καταλείπειν. πρὸ τρίτης οὖν ἡμέρας τοῦ πάθους αὐτῶν κοινῷ στεναγμῷ ἑνωθέντες προσευχὴν πρὸς τὸν Κύριον ἐποιήσαντο· καὶ εὐθὺς μετὰ τὴν προσευχὴν ὠδῖνες

C. XIV., l. 11. ὁ θεος deest.   13. σαρκα· cod. ψυχην.   ψυχην· cod. σαρκα.
C. XV., l. 17. πανοδυρετο.

---

essentially from τοὺς μάρτυράς γε, i.e. 'the martyrs were there, if none others.' In that case Tertullian has made the suggestion a little more definite. Or we may conjecture that the primitive Greek text to which Tertullian is referring read ἀλλάγε καὶ τούτους μάρτυρας, which scarcely differs from our edited text.

But it is conceivable that, after all, Tertullian is referring to the earlier part of the vision where Iucundus, and Artaxius are seen beyond the plain. Perhaps this last group of nameless brethren are not in Paradise at all; Aspasius and Optatus at all events are still alive.

In Perpetua's own vision in c. IV. the white-robed throng correspond to the company in the Apocalypse who have come up out of the great tribulation. They are therefore martyrs.

C. XIV. εἰ καὶ μὴ τὴν σάρκα. The scribe supposing that Secundus was *killed* in the prison, assumes of course that the sword did pierce his flesh, and not his soul: thus the obvious allusion to the Gospel of Luke is weakened; and the sentence deprived of its meaning. We have restored the order against the MS.

invaserunt. Et cum, pro naturali difficultate octavi mensis, in partu laborans doloret, ait illi quidam ex ministris cataractariorum: Quae sic modo doles, quid facies objecta bestiis, quas contemsisti cum sacrificare noluisti? Et illa respondit: *Modo ego patior quod patior, illic autem alius erit in me qui patietur pro me, quia et ego pro illo passura sum.* Ita enixa est puellam, quam sibi quaedam soror in filiam educavit.

XVI. Quoniam ergo permisit, et permittendo voluit Spiritus sanctus ordinem ipsius muneris conscribi, etsi indigni ad supplementum tantae gloriae describendum, tamen quasi mandatum sanctissimae Perpetuae, immo fidei commissum eius exsequimur, unum adicientes documentum de ipsius constantia et animi sublimitate. Cum[1] a tribuno castigatius eo tractarentur; quia ex admonitionibus hominum vanissimorum verebatur, ne subtraherentur de carcere incantationibus aliquibus magicis; in faciem respondit Perpetua, et dixit: Quid utique non permittis refrigerare noxiis nobilissimis, Caesaris scilicet, et natali[2] eiusdem pugnaturis? Aut non tua gloria est, si pinguiores illo producamur? Horruit et erubuit tribunus; et ita iussit illos humanius haberi, ut fratribus eius et ceteris facultas fieret introeundi, et refrigerandi cum eis; iam et[3] ipso Optione carceris credente.

XVII. Pridie quoque cum illa coena ultima, quam liberam vocant, quantum in ipsis erat non coenam liberam, sed agapen coenarent, eadem constantia ad populum verba ista iactabant, comminantes iudicium Domini, contestantes passioni suae felicitatem, inridentes[4] concurrentium curiositatem, dicente Saturo: Crastinus dies satis vobis non est, quod libenter videtis quod odistis, hodie amici, cras inimici. Notate tamen nobis[5] facies

---

[1] S and C, quia tribuno castigante eos et male tractante, quoniam ex admonitionibus.

[2] S and C, quia natali eius sumus pugnaturi.   [3] H, tamen.

[4] H, irritantes.   [5] S, vobis.

C. xv. ἐκεῖ δὲ ἄλλος. Cf. *Acta S. Victoris* (Ruinart p. 260), "Ego sum, inquit, Jesus qui in sanctis meis iniurias et tormenta sustineo."

C. xvi. This seems to be imitated in *Acta S. Montani* (Ruinart p. 204), "Haec omnes de carcere simul scripserant. Sed quia necesse erat omnem actum martyrum beatorum pleno sermone complecti; quia et ipsi de se per modestiam minus dixerant: et Flavianus quoque privatim hoc nobis munus iniunxit ut quicquid litteris eorum deesset, adderemus etc."

C. xvii. The 'last supper' of the criminals is referred to by Tertullian, *Apol.* 42, "Non in publico Liberalibus discumbo, quod bestiariis supremam

ΜΑΡΤΥΡΙΟΝ ΠΕΡΠΕΤΟΥΑC. 61

αὐτὴν συνέσχον, κατὰ τὴν τοῦ ὀγδόου μηνὸς φύσιν χαλεπαί. καὶ μετὰ τοῦ τοκετοῦ καμοῦσα ἤλγει. ἔφη δέ τις αὐτῇ τῶν παρατηρούντων ὑπηρετῶν· Εἰ νῦν οὕτως ἀλγεῖς τί ἔχεις ποιῆσαι, βληθεῖσα πρὸς θηρία ὧν κατεφρόνησας ὅτε ἐπιθύειν κατεφρόνησας καὶ οὐκ ἠθέλησας θῦσαι; κἀκείνη ἀπεκρίθη· 5 Νῦν ἐγὼ πάσχω ὃ πάσχω· ἐκεῖ δὲ ἄλλος ἐστὶν ὁ πάσχων ὑπὲρ ἐμοῦ· ἔσται ἐν ἐμοὶ ἵνα πάθῃ διότι ἐγὼ πάσχω ὑπὲρ αὐτοῦ.

Ἔτεκεν δὲ κοράσιον ὃ μία τῶν ἀδελφῶν συλλαβοῦσα εἰς θυγατέρα ἀνέθρεψεν αὐτῇ.

XVI. Ἡμῖν δὲ ἀναξίοις οὖσιν ἐπέτρεψεν τὸ ἅγιον πνεῦμα 10 ἀναγράψαι τὴν τάξιν τὴν ἐπὶ ταῖς φιλοτιμίαις παρακολουθήσασαν· πλὴν ὡς ἐντάλματι τῆς μακαρίας Περπετούας μᾶλλον δὲ ὡς κελεύσματι ὑπηρετοῦντες ἀναπληροῦμεν τὸ προσταχθὲν ἡμῖν. Ὡς δὲ πλείους ἡμέραι διεγίνοντο ἐν τῇ φυλακῇ ὄντων αὐτῶν, ἡ μεγαλόφρων καὶ ἀνδρεία ὡς ἀληθῶς Περπετούα, τοῦ 15 χιλιάρχου ἀπεινέστερον αὐτοῖς προσφερομένου, τινῶν πρὸς αὐτὸν ματαίως διαβεβαιωσαμένων τὸ δεῖν φοβεῖσθαι μήπως ἐπῳδαῖς μαγικαῖς τῆς φυλακῆς ὑπεξέλθωσιν, ἐνώπιον ἀπεκρίθη λέγουσα· Διατί ἡμῖν ἀναλαμβάνειν οὐκ ἐπιτρέπεις ὀνομαστοῖς καταδίκοις Καίσαρος γενεθλίοις ἀναλωθησομένοις; μὴ γὰρ οὐχὶ 20 σὴ δόξα ἐστίν, ἐφ' ὅσον πίονες προσερχόμεθα; πρὸς ταῦτα ἔφριξε καὶ ἐδυσωπήθη ὁ χιλίαρχος, ἐκέλευσέν τε αὐτοὺς φιλανθρωπότερον διάγειν, ὡς καὶ τὸν ἀδελφὸν αὐτῆς καὶ λοιπούς τινας δεδυνῆσθαι εἰσελθεῖν καὶ ἀναλαμβάνειν μετ' αὐτῶν. τότε καὶ αὐτὸς ὁ τῆς φυλακῆς προεστὼς ἐπίστευσεν. 25

XVII. Ἀλλὰ καὶ πρὸ μιᾶς ὅτε τὸ ἔσχατον ἐκεῖνο δεῖπνον ὅπερ ἐλεύθερον ὀνομάζουσιν· ὅσον δὲ ἐφ' ἑαυτοῖς οὐκ ἐλεύθερον δεῖπνον ἀλλ' ἀγάπην ἐπεκάλουν τῇ αὐτῶν παρρησίᾳ· πρὸς δὲ τὸν ὄχλον τὸν ἐκεῖσε παρεστῶτα ῥήματα ἐξέπεμπον μετὰ πολλῆς παρρησίας αὐτοῖς ἀπειλοῦντες κρίσιν Θεοῦ, ἀνθομο- 30 λογούμενοι τὸν μακαρισμὸν τοῦ πάθους ἑαυτῶν, καταγελῶντες τὴν περιεργείαν τῶν συντρεχόντων, Σατύρου λέγοντος· Ἡ αὔριον ἡμέρα ὑμῖν οὐκ ἐπαρκεῖ; τί ἡδέως ὁρᾶτε οὓς μισεῖτε· σήμερον φίλοι· αὔριον ἐχθροί; πλὴν ἐπισημειώσασθε τὰ πρόσωπα ἡμῶν ἐπιμελῶς ἵνα καὶ ἐπιγνῶτε ἡμᾶς ἐν ἐκείνῃ τῇ ἡμέρᾳ. 35

1. Cod. φυσι.   2. του τοκετου.   C. xvi., l. 15. ει μεγαλοφρον.
21. cod. πλειορες.   C. xvii., l. 32. λεγοντος· cod. λεωντος.   33. υμιν·
cod. ημιν.   μισειτε. cod. μασῆται.

---

coenantibus mos est." It appears then that the *free* supper was originally a supper in honour of Bacchus.

nostras diligenter, ut recognoscatis nos in die illo iudicii. Ita omnes[1] inde attoniti discedebant: ex quibus multi crediderunt.

XVIII. Inluxit dies victoriae illorum, et processerunt de carcere in amphitheatrum, quasi in caelum, hilares, vultu decori; si forte, gaudio paventes non timore. Sequebatur Perpetua placido vultu[2], et pedum incessu, ut matrona Christi Dei dilecta: vigore oculorum deiciens omnium conspectum. Item Felicitas salvam se peperisse gaudens ut ad bestias pugnaret, a sanguine, ab obstetrice ad retiarium, lotura post partum baptismo secundo. Et cum delati[3] essent in portam, et cogerentur habitum induere; viri quidem sacerdotum Saturni, feminae vero sacratarum Cereri; generosa illa in finem usque constantia repugnavit. Dicebant enim: Ideo ad hoc sponte pervenimus, ne libertas nostra abduceretur. Ideo animas nostras addiximus, ne tale aliquid faceremus: hoc vobiscum pacti sumus. Agnovit iniustitia iustitiam: concessit tribunus, ut quomodo erant, simpliciter inducerentur. Perpetua psallebat, caput iam Aegyptii calcans. Revocatus et Saturninus et Saturus populo spectanti comminabantur de hoc. Ut sub conspectu Hilariani pervenerunt, gestu et nutu coeperunt

[1] S, multi.
[2] H, lucido vultu ut matrona Christi, ut Dei delicata, vigore oculorum deiciens omnium conspectum. Ed., placido vultu, et pedum incessu, ut matrona Christi Dei dilecta: vigorem oculorum suorum deiciens ab omnium conspectu.
[3] H, ducti.

C. XVIII. ἐπέλαμψεν. Imitated in *Passio Cypriani* p. 186, "illuxit denique dies alius, ille signatus, ille promissus ille divinus...dies de conscientia futuri martyris laetus."

ὡς εἰς οὐρανόν. Imitated in *Acta Montani*, "ad summum ascendebamus locum poenarum quasi ascenderemus in caelum."

ὡς ματρῶνα Χριστοῦ. So Blandina is described in the Lyons martyrdoms: ὡς εἰς νυμφικὸν δεῖπνον κεκλημένη ἀλλὰ μὴ πρὸς θηρία βεβλημένη. Cf. Tert. *ad uxor.* i. 4, "Sorores nostrae...malunt Deo nubere."

ἠναγκάζοντο κτέ. From Tertullian, *De Testim. Animae* 2, we find that the men would have been dressed in scarlet cloaks, while the women would have worn a fillet round their heads. "Unde hoc tibi non Christianae? atque id plerumque et vitta Cereris redimita, et pallio Saturni coccinata." Cf. also *De Pallio* 4. It was apparently not an uncommon thing to make the Christian convict represent some mythological character or to engage in some idolatrous ceremony. Thus Clement in his epistle speaks of Christian women who played the part of the Danaids or of Dirce in the arena. In the Acts of Theodotus (Ruinart p. 301) we have a case of persons who were made priests of Diana and Minerva: "iussit eas fieri Dianae et Minervae sacerdotes ut quotannis iuxta morem lavarent earum simulacra in vicino lacu."

In our Acts the allusion to priests of Kronos and priestesses of Demeter is

ΜΑΡΤΥΡΙΟΝ ΠΕΡΠΕΤΟΥΑC.

Οὕτως ἅπαντες ἐκεῖθεν ἐκπληττόμενοι ἐχωρίζοντο, ἐξ ὧν πλεῖστοι ἐπίστευσαν.

XVIII. Ἐπέλαμψε δὲ ἡ ἡμέρα τῆς νίκης αὐτῶν· καὶ προῆλθον ἐκ τῆς φυλακῆς εἰς τὸ ἀμφιθέατρον ὡς εἰς οὐρανὸν ἀπιόντες, ἱλαροὶ καὶ φαιδροὶ τῷ προσώπῳ, πτοούμενοι εἰ τύχοι χαρᾷ μᾶλλον ἢ φόβῳ.

Ἠκολούθη δὲ ἡ Περπετούα πράως βαδίζουσα, ὡς ματρώνα Χριστοῦ, ἐγρηγόρῳ ὀφθαλμῷ, καὶ τῇ προσόψει καταβάλλουσα τὰς πάντων ὁράσεις.

Ὁμοίως καὶ ἡ Φηλικητάτη χαίρουσα ἐπὶ τῇ τοῦ τοκετοῦ ὑγείᾳ ἵνα θηριομαχήσῃ, ἀπὸ αἵματος εἰς αἷμα, ἀπὸ μαίας πρὸς μονομαχίαν, μέλλουσα λούσασθαι μετὰ τὸν τοκετόν, βαπτισμῷ δὲ ὑστέρῳ τουτέστι τῷ ἰδίῳ αἵματι.

Ὅτε δὲ ἤγγισαν πρὸ τοῦ ἀμφιθεάτρου, ἠναγκάζοντο ἐνδύσασθαι σχήματα, οἱ μὲν ἄρρενες ἱερέων Κρόνου, αἱ δὲ θηλεῖαι τῆς Δημήτρας· ἀλλ' ἡ εὐγενεστάτη ἐκείνη Περπετούα παρρησίᾳ ἠγωνίσατο ἕως τέλους· ἔλεγεν γάρ· Διὰ τοῦτο ἑκουσίως εἰς τοῦτο ἐληλύθαμεν· ἵνα ἡ ἐλευθερία ἡμῶν μὴ ἡττηθῇ· διὰ τοῦτο τὴν ψυχὴν ἡμῶν παρεδώκαμεν ἵνα μηδὲν τῶν τοιούτων πράξωμεν· τοῦτο συνεταξάμεθα μεθ' ὑμῶν.

Ἐπέγνω ἡ ἀδικία τὴν δικαιοσύνην· καὶ μετέπειτα ἐπέτρεψεν ὁ χιλίαρχος ἵνα οὕτως εἰσαχθῶσιν ὡς ἦσαν· καὶ ἡ Περπετούα ἔψαλλεν, τὴν κεφαλὴν τοῦ Αἰγυπτίου ἤδη πατοῦσα.

Ῥεουκᾶτος δὲ καὶ Σατουρνῖνος καὶ Σάτυρος τῷ θεωροῦντι ὄχλῳ προσωμίλουν· καὶ γενόμενοι ἔμπροσθεν Ἱλαριάνου, κινή-

C. xviii., l. 5. η τυχοι. 20. cod. τουτο συνεταξωμεθα μεθασυνεταξεσθαι μεθ' υμων (sic). 24. Σατουρνιλος. 25. προσομηλουν: (Lat. προσηπειλουν).

---

thoroughly in harmony with the evidence supplied by North African inscriptions. The cultus was one which not only was appropriate to the older rural life, and to the Punic settlers who inherited Phenician forms of idolatry, but in the great wheat raising districts would hold its own against any pressure of recently imported religions. Thus we find *C. I. L.* VIII. 2266, FRUGIFERO SATURNO AUG. SAC. TI. TELTONIUS MARCELLUS PRAEFEC. LEG. III. AUG. P. V. V.S.L.A. and 4581, DEO FRUGUM. SATURNO FRUGIFERO &c.

The African references to the priesthood attached to the worship of Saturn and Ceres are numerous. Nine inscriptions commemorate priests of Ceres, and of these seven are women: over thirty inscriptions record the names of priests of Saturn. No other form of African worship is so well represented by memorials of its officials as these are. The whole number of Ceres-inscriptions is about twenty, of Saturn one hundred and five. Not even Jupiter is so frequent as this last. It may be said, therefore, that the allusion made in the Acts to the worship of Saturn and Ceres is in harmony with the evidence of inscriptions which makes them to be amongst the most popular of African deities. Temples of Ceres are

Hilariano dicere: Tu nos, inquiunt, te autem Deus iudicabit. Ad hoc populus exasperatus, flagellis eos vexari pro ordine venatorum postulavit. Et utique illi gratulati, quod aliquid et de dominicis passionibus essent consecuti.

XIX. Sed qui dixerat, Petite et accipietis, petentibus dedit eum exitum, quem quisque desideraverat. Nam si quando inter se de martyrii sui voto sermocinabantur, Saturninus quidem omnibus bestiis velle se obici profitebatur: ut scilicet gloriosiorem gestaret coronam. Itaque in commissione spectaculi, ipse et Revocatus leopardum experti, etiam super pulpitum ab urso vexati sunt. Saturus autem nihil magis quam ursum abominabatur: sed uno morsu leopardi confici se iam praesumebat. Itaque cum aper subministraretur, venator potius qui illum apro subministraverat[1], subfossus ab eadem bestia, post dies muneris obiit. Saturus solummodo tractus est. Et cum ad ursum substrictus esset in ponte, ursus de cavea prodire noluit. Itaque secundo Saturus inlaesus revocatur.

XX. Puellis autem ferocissimam vaccam, ideoque praeter consuetudinem comparatam[2], diabolus praeparavit: sexui earum etiam de bestia aemulatus. Itaque despoliatae et reticulis indutae[3] producebantur. Horruit populus, alteram respiciens puellam delicatam, alteram a partu recenti stillantibus mammis. Ita revocatae[4] et discinctis indutae. Inducitur prior Perpetua; iactata est, et

[1] H, apro subligaverat. Ed., aprum subministraverat.
[2] H, paratam.   [3] S and C, dispoliatae promovebantur.
[4] Ed., revocatae discinguntur.

noted by the inscriptions at Agbia in Proconsular Africa and at Theveste in Numidia; at Sitifis in Mauretania have been found inscriptions in honor both of Saturn and Ceres. Cf. *C. I. L.* VIII. 8442—8450.

But beyond the fact that the worship of Ceres and of Saturn was popular in Africa, there was a special reason for attempting to dress them this way. We have shewn on p. 5, that the dedicated priestesses of Ceres were women who had left their husbands; and the populace would not be slow in seeing the appropriateness of the raiment to the case. Still more fun would be made of the men; for as priests of Saturn, who devoured children, they would furnish an excellent reminder of the scandals which prevailed as to the Thyestean banquets of the Christians, and their custom of eating in secret "the flesh of the Son of man and drinking his blood"; we may be sure that when the scarlet robes of the priests of Saturn appeared in the arena a shout of delight would have passed round the benches where the expectant Carthaginian populace were seated.

To modern Christians these allusions are valuable because they shew us an historical nucleus of the shameful blood-scandals against the Jews, and because they are in evidence for the early diffusion of the language of the fourth

μασιν καὶ νεύμασιν ἔφασαν· Σὺ ἡμᾶς καὶ σὲ ὁ θεός. πρὸς ταῦτα ἀγριωθεὶς ὁ ὄχλος μαστιγωθῆναι αὐτοὺς ἐβόησεν· ἀλλὰ οἱ ἅγιοι ἠγαλλιάσθησαν ὅτι ὑπέμεινάν τι καὶ τῶν κυριακῶν παθῶν.

XIX. Ἀλλ' ὁ εἰπών· Αἰτεῖσθε καὶ λήψεσθε, ἔδωκεν τοῖς αἰτήσασιν ταύτην τὴν δόξαν οἵαν ἕκαστος αὐτῶν ἐπεθύμησεν. εἴποτε γὰρ μεθ' ἑαυτῶν περὶ τῆς εὐχῆς τοῦ μαρτυρίου συνελάλουν, Σατουρνῖνος μὲν πᾶσιν τοῖς θηρίοις βληθῆναι ἑαυτὸν ἔθελεν πάντως ἵνα ἐνδοξότερον στέφανον ἀπολάβῃ. ἐν ἀρχῇ γοῦν τῆς θεωρίας αὐτὸς μετὰ Ῥεουκάτου πάρδαλιν ὑπέμεινεν· ἀλλὰ καὶ ὕστερον ἐπὶ τῆς γεφύρας ὑπὸ ἄρκου διεσπαράχθη. Σάτυρος δὲ οὐδὲν ἄλλο ἢ ἄρκον ἀπεστρέφετο· καὶ ἑνὶ δήγματι παρδάλεως τελειοῦσθαι αὐτὸν ἐπεπόθει· ὥστε καὶ τῷ συΐ *διακονούμενος* ἐσύρη μόνον, σχοινίῳ προσδεθείς· ὁ δὲ θηρατὴς ὁ τῷ συῒ αὐτὸν προσβαλὼν ὑπὸ θηρὸς κατετρώθη οὕτως ὡς μεθ' ἡμέραν τῶν φιλοτιμιῶν ἀποθανεῖν. ἀλλὰ καὶ πρὸς ἄρκον διαδεθεὶς ὑγιὴς πάλιν διέμεινεν· ἐκ γὰρ τοῦ ζωγρίου αὐτῆς ἡ ἄρκος οὐκ ἐθέλησεν ἐξελθεῖν.

XX. Ταῖς μακαρίαις δὲ νεάνισιν ἀγριωτάτην δάμαλιν ἡτοίμασεν ὁ διάβολος, τὸ θῆλυ αὐτῶν παραζηλῶν διὰ τοῦ θηρίου· καὶ γυμνωθεῖσαι γοῦν προσήγοντο· ὅθεν ἀπεστράφη ὁ ὄχλος, μίαν μὲν τρυφερὰν κόρην βλέπων, τὴν δὲ ἄλλην μασθοὺς στάζουσαν γάλα, ὡς προσφάτως κυήσασαν· καὶ ἀναληφθεῖσαι πάλιν, καὶ δικτύοις περιβληθεῖσαι, ἐνδιδύσκονται ὑποζώσμασιν· ὅθεν εἰσελθουσῶν αὐτῶν, ἡ Περπετούα πρώτη κερατισθεῖσα

C. xix., l. 8. Σατουρνιλος.   9. θελειν.   13. επεποθη.   17. διεμεινον.
C. xx., 22. μασθοις.

---

gospel; they furnish us, therefore, with materials upon which to base acts of repentance and of faith.

C. xix. διακονούμενος: is this for δεικνύμενος?

σχοινίῳ προσδεθείς. The martyr was attached by a rope to the wild beast, before it was loosed from its den, in order that he might not escape. This explains why in some of the more famous martyrdoms the saints have pulled the beasts towards them: for example in the letter of the Smyrnaeans on the death of Polycarp, we are told that Germanicus ἑαυτῷ τὸ θηρίον ἐπεσπάσατο προσβιασάμενος. And in Euseb. H. E. viii. 7 the martyrs are said to do the very same thing, τῶν ἱερῶν ἀθλητῶν γυμνῶν ἑστώτων καὶ ταῖς χερσὶ κατασειόντων ἐπί τε σφᾶς αὐτοὺς ἐπισπωμένων. Lightfoot quotes these passages in illustration of Ign. ad Rom. v. 5 (προσβιάσομαι) but does not notice that the force is applied by means of a rope.

C. xx. δικτύοις περιβληθεῖσα. The whole incident recalls the martyrdom of Blandina τοὔσχατον εἰς γυργαθὸν βληθεῖσα, ταύρῳ παρεβλήθη.

concidit in lumbos. Et ut conspexit[1] tunicam a latere discissam, ad velamentum femorum adduxit, pudoris potius memor, quam doloris. Dehinc requisita, et dispersos capillos infibulavit. Non enim decebat Martyrem dispersis capillis pati, ne in sua gloria plangere videretur. Ita surrexit, et elisam Felicitatem cum vidisset, accessit, et manum ei tradidit et sublevavit illam. Et ambae pariter steterunt, et populi duritia devicta revocatae sunt in portam Sanavivariam. Illic Perpetua a quodam tunc catechumino, Rustico nomine, qui ei adhaerebat, suscepta, et quasi a somno expergita (adeo in Spiritu et in ecstasi fuerat) circumspicere coepit, et stupentibus omnibus ait: Quando, inquit, producimur ad vaccam illam nescio quam[2]? Et cum audisset quod iam evenerat, non prius credidit, nisi quasdam notas vexationis in corpore et habitu suo recognovisset[3]. Exinde accersitum fratrem suum, et illum catechuminum allocuta est eos, dicens; In fide state, et invicem omnes diligite; et passionibus nostris ne scandalizemini.

XXI. Item Saturus in alia porta militem Pudentem[4] exhortabatur dicens ad summum[5]; sicut promisi et praedixi, nullam usque adhuc bestiam sensi. Et nunc de toto corde credas. Ecce prodeo illo, et ab uno morsu leopardi consumar. Et statim in fine spectaculi, leopardo obiectus de uno morsu eius tanto perfusus est sanguine, ut populus revertenti illi secundi baptismatis testimonium reclamaverit: Salvum lotum, salvum lotum. Plane

[1] H, ubi sedit.
[2] Sic S and C, in Ed. deest *quam*.
[3] Ed. addit *et illum catechuminum*.
[4] In H deest *Pudentem*.
[5] Sic H, Ed. habet *adsum certe*.

της δὲ σκληρότητος. Cf. *Passio Cypriani* p. 196, "victa denique feritate torquentium."

C. XXI. ἐνεπλήσθη. Cf. Dion Cass. LXXVII. 2 καὶ γὰρ τοῦ αἵματος πᾶσα ἐπλήσθη, where Geta is massacred in his mother's arms.

καλῶς ἐλούσω. Aubé remarks that it is quite possible that no one except the author of the Acts saw an allusion to Christian baptism (much less to the Montanistic idea of martyrdom as a second baptism), in the cry of the populace. And he refers to an inscription at Brescia to shew that the expression is simply a bath-motto. In this inscription (*C. I. L.* v. 4500) the mosaic of an ancient bath pavement furnishes us with the following formulae proper to the occasion;

| BENE | SALVV | PERIPSV |
| LAVA | LOTVM | MA SV |

or 'bene lava,' 'salvum lotum,' 'peripsema sume.' The second of these is the formula in our Acts; its proper Greek equivalent is 'καλῶς ἐλούσω,' and it is addressed to a person when leaving the bath. The *Corpus Inscriptionum* shews

ΜΑΡΤΥΡΙΟΝ ΠΕΡΠΕΤΟΥΑC. 67

ἔπεσεν ἐπ' ὀσφύος· καὶ ἀνακαθίσασα τὸν χιτῶνα ἐκ τῆς πλευρᾶς αὐτῆς συναγαγοῦσα, ἐσκέπασεν τὸν ἑαυτῆς μηρόν, αἰδοῦς μᾶλλον μνημονεύσασα ἢ πόνων· [αἰδουμένη·] μηδαμῶς φροντίσασα τῶν ἀλγηδόνων· καὶ ἐπιζητήσασα βελόνην τὰ ἐσπαραγμένα συνέσφιγξεν, καὶ τὰς τρίχας τῆς κεφαλῆς περι- 5 έδησεν· (οὐ γὰρ ἔπρεπεν τῇ μάρτυρι θριξὶν σπαραχθείσαις ὁρᾶσθαι· ἵνα μὴ ἐν τῇ ἰδίᾳ τιμῇ δοκῇ πενθεῖν.)

[Καὶ κερατισθεῖσαν ἰδοῦσα τὴν Φηλικητάτην, προσῆλθεν αὐτῇ] καὶ κρατήσασα τῆς χειρὸς αὐτῆς ἤγειρεν αὐτήν. καὶ ἔστησαν ἅμα· τῆς δὲ σκληρότητος τοῦ ὄχλου ἐκνικηθείσης 10 ἀνελήφθησαν εἰς τὴν πύλην τὴν ζωτικήν· ἐκεῖ ἡ Περπετούα ὑπό τινος κατηχουμένου ὀνόματι Ῥουστίκου ὃς παρειστήκει αὐτῇ ὡς ἐξ ὕπνου ἐγερθεῖσα (οὕτως ἐν πνεύματι γέγονεν ἔκστασιν παθοῦσα), καὶ περιβλεψαμένη θαμβούντων ἁπάντων ἔφη· Πότε βαλλόμεθα πρὸς τὴν δάμαλιν ἣν λέγουσιν; καὶ 15 ἀκούσασα ὅτι ἤδη ἐξεληλύθει πρὸς αὐτήν, οὐ πρότερον ἐπίστευσεν πρὶν ἢ σημεῖά τινα τῆς βλάβης ἐν τῷ ἰδίῳ σώματι ἑωράκει· ἀναδειχθέντων δὲ καλέσασα τὸν ἴδιον ἀδελφὸν καὶ αὐτὸν τὸν κατηχούμενον παρεκάλει ἵνα ἐν πίστει διαμείνωσιν καὶ ἀλλήλους ἀγαπῶσιν, καὶ τοῖς παθήμασιν ἐκείνοις μὴ 20 σκανδαλισθῶσιν τοιούτοις οὖσιν.

XXI. Καὶ ἐν ἑτέρᾳ πύλῃ ὁ Σάτυρος τῷ στρατιώτῃ Πούδεντι προσομίλει, καθόλου λέγων ὅτι, Κατὰ τὴν πρόλεξιν τὴν ἐμήν, ὡς καὶ προεῖπον, οὐδὲ ἓν θηρίων ἥψατό μου ἕως ἄρτι· ἰδοὺ δὲ νῦν, ἵνα ἐξ ὅλης καρδίας διαπιστεύσῃς, προσέρχομαι, καὶ ἐν ἑνὶ 25 δήγματι παρδάλεως τελειοῦμαι· καὶ εὐθὺς ἐν τέλει τῆς θεωρίας πάρδαλις αὐτῷ ἐβλήθη, καὶ ἐν ἑνὶ δήγματι τοῦ αἵματος τοῦ ἁγίου ἐνεπλήσθη· τοσοῦτον [δὴ] αἷμα ἐρρύη, ὡς λογισθῆναι δευτέρου βαπτισμοῦ μαρτύριον· καθὼς καὶ ἐπεφώνει ὁ ὄχλος βοῶν καὶ λέγων· Καλῶς ἐλούσω· καλῶς ἐλούσω. καὶ μὴν 30 ὑγιὴς ἦν ὁ τοιούτῳ τρόπῳ λελουμένος.

1. cod. κρατηθησα (sic). 3. αιδου. 6. σπαραχθησαν. 7. δωκει. 8. cod. om. [ ] transiliens a κερατισθεισαν ad κρατησασα. 18. αναδειχθησασα. C. XXI., l. 26. δειγματι. 27. δειγματι. 28. ερυει. 29. δευτερον. επεφωνη.

---

this by a reference to Haupt: "in colloquiis quae ex codice Montepessulano 306 (saec. IX) nuper edidit Hauptius in indice lectionum univ. Berolinensis m. Oct. a. 1871, p. 8, καλῶς ἔλουσον (scr. ἐλούσω) κύριε, salvum lutum (sic) domine." Aubé gives the equivalent καλῶς ἔλουσον and refers to *Notices et Extraits des MSS.* XXIII. p. 322, where the spelling would seem to imply that this is the same MS. as quoted

utique salvus erat, qui hoc modo laverat[1]. Tunc Pudenti militi: Vale, inquit, et memor esto fidei meae; et haec te non conturbent, sed confirment. Simulque ansulam[2] de digito eius petiit, et vulneri suo mersam reddidit ei, beatam hereditatem, relinquens ei pignus et memoriam tanti sanguinis[3]. Exinde iam exanimis prosternitur cum ceteris ad iugulationem solito loco. Et cum populus illos in medium postularet, ut gladio penetrante in eorum corpore oculos suos comites homicidii adiungeret; ultro surrexerunt, et se quo volebat populus transtulerunt: ante iam osculati invicem, ut martyrium per solemnia pacis consummarent. Ceteri quidem immobiles, et cum silentio ferrum receperunt: multo magis Saturus: qui et prior scalam ascenderat, prior reddidit spiritum, nam et Perpetuam sustinebat. Perpetua autem, ut aliquid doloris gustaret, inter ossa compuncta[4] exululavit; et errantem dexteram tirunculi gladiatoris ipsa in iugulum suum posuit[5]. Fortasse tanta femina aliter non potuisset occidi: quia ab immundo timebatur, nisi ipsa voluisset.

O fortissimi ac beatissimi Martyres! O vere vocati et electi in gloriam Domini nostri Iesu Christi; quem qui magnificat, et honorificat, et adorat, utique et haec non minus veteribus exempla in aedificationem Ecclesiae legere debet, ut novae quoque virtutes unum et eundem semper Spiritum sanctum usque adhuc operari testificentur; et omnipotentem Deum Patrem et Filium eius Iesum Christum Dominum nostrum, cui est claritas et immensa potestas in Saecula Saeculorum. Amen.

[1] Sic H, Ed. spectaculo claruerat.   [2] S, anulum.
[3] Sic S, Ed. habet *reddidit ei*, hereditatem pignoris relinquens illi, et memoriam sanguinis.
[4] Sic H, Ed. costas puncta.   [5] H, transtulit.

---

by Haupt. As to the third formula, we have given 'peripsema sume,' i.e. 'take a towel,' as suggested by Haupt; but it is an open question whether it is not really a transliteration of περίψημά σου ('your devoted servant'); the three sentences on the mosaic being thus three forms of address to the person bathed by the bathman. The use of such conventional formulae is well illustrated by Oriental life; as for instance in the case of shaving where the barber concludes his task by the words "may God make it agreeable to you."

A similar inscription in mosaic is given amongst the inscriptions from Mauretania (C. I. L. VIII. 2, no. 8424. Cf. additamenta in p. 970): which may be read as follows: *bene laves: oze = (hodie) a[ssem] des, cras gratis: res tuta. Salvu[s] laves et bono [eius] q[u]i fieri jussit ex s[uo parcimonio]*. One would imagine therefore that it was a common thing to work such devices into the mosaics of baths.

καὶ δακτύλιον αἰτήσας. The optiones of the legion all wore rings: thus we have in C. I. L. VIII. 2554 an inscription from the camp at Lambaesis where the

ΜΑΡΤΥΡΙΟΝ ΠΕΡΠΕΤΟΥΑΣ. 69

Τότε τῷ στρατιώτῃ Πούδεντι ἔφη· Ὑγίαινε καὶ μνημόνευε πίστεως καὶ ἐμοῦ· καὶ τὰ τοιαῦτα καὶ στερεωσάτω σε μᾶλλον ἢ ταραξάτω.

Καὶ δακτύλιον αἰτήσας παρ' αὐτοῦ καὶ ἐνθεὶς αὐτὸ τῷ ἰδίῳ αἵματι ἔδωκεν αὐτῷ μακαρίαν κληρονομίαν, ἀφεὶς μνήμην καὶ ἐνθήκην αἵματος τηλικούτου. μετὰ ταῦτα λοιπὸν ἐμπνέων ἔτι ἀπήχθη μετὰ καὶ τῶν ἄλλων τῷ συνήθει τόπῳ· εἰς σφαγὴν δὲ ὁ ὄχλος ᾔτησεν αὐτοὺς εἰς μέσον μεταχθῆναι, ὅπως διὰ τῶν ἁγίων σωμάτων ἐλαυνόμενον τὸ ξίφος θεάσωνται· καὶ οἱ μακάριοι μάρτυρες ἑκόντες ἠγέρθησαν· ᾐσχύνοντο γὰρ ὀλίγους μάρτυρας ἔχειν ἐπὶ τῷ μακαρίῳ θανάτῳ αὐτῶν.

Καὶ δὴ ἐλθόντων αὐτῶν ὅπου ὁ ὄχλος ἐβούλετο πρῶτον κατεφίλησαν ἀλλήλους ἵνα τὸ μυστήριον διὰ τῶν οἰκείων τῆς πίστεως τελειώσωσιν· καὶ μετέπειτα ἀσμένως ὑπέμειναν τὴν διὰ τοῦ ξίφους τιμωρίαν· πολλῷ δὲ μᾶλλον ὁ Σάτυρος, ὁ δὴ πρότερος τὴν κλίμακα ἐκείνην ἀναβάς, ὃς καὶ ἔπεισεν τὴν Περπετούαν ἀναβαίνειν.

Ἡ δὲ Περπετούα ἵνα καὶ αὐτὴ γεύσηται τῶν πόνων περὶ τὰ ὀστέα νυγεῖσα ἠλάλαξεν, καὶ πεπλανημένην τὴν δεξιὰν ἀπείρου μονομάχου κρατήσασα προσήγαγεν τῇ κατακλεῖδι ἑαυτῆς· ἴσως τὴν τοσαύτην γυναῖκα τοῦ ἀκαθάρτου πνεύματος φοβουμένου [φονεῦσαι], φονευθῆναι μὴ βουλομένην.

Ὦ ἀνδριώτατοι καὶ μακαριώτατοι μάρτυρες καὶ στρατιῶται ἐκλεκτοί, εἰς δόξαν Κυρίου Ἰησοῦ Χριστοῦ κεκλημένοι. πῶς μεγαλύνωμεν ὑμᾶς ἢ μακαρίσωμεν, γενναιότατοι στρατιῶται; οὐκ ἧσσον τῶν παλαιῶν γραφῶν, ἃ εἰς οἰκοδομὴν ἐκκλησίας [ἀναγινώσκεται,] ἀναγινώσκεσθαι ὀφείλει ἡ πανάρετος πολιτεία τῶν μακαρίων μαρτύρων * * * * * δι' ὧν δόξαν ἀναπέμπομεν τῷ πατρὶ τῶν αἰώνων, ἅμα τῷ μονογενεῖ αὐτοῦ υἱῷ τῷ Κυρίῳ ἡμῶν Ἰησοῦ Χριστῷ σὺν ἁγίῳ πνεύματι· ᾧ ἡ δόξα καὶ τὸ κράτος εἰς τοὺς αἰῶνας τῶν αἰώνων. Ἀμήν.

1. Πουδεντιω. 7. εισφαγην (sic). 9. θεασονται. 10. ισχυνοντο.
12. και δει. 14. ασμενος. 16. ως και εφησεν. 18. πεπλανημενη.
19. κατακληδη. 20. του· cod. υπο. 21. cod. om. φονευσαι. cod. και φονευθηναι μη βουλομενον. 25. ισον. 26. cod. om. αναγινωσκεται.
27. desunt quaedam: cf. Lat.

formation of a college and the foundation of a schola by the optiones of one of the legions: there are sixty of these optiones corresponding to the sixty centurions: the concluding part of the inscription (veterani quoque missi accipiant kal. Jan. anularium) decrees that all the discharged veterans should receive a ring on the Kalends of January. Pudens' ring is probably something of the same kind.

πεπλανημένην. Cf. *Passio Cypriani* 186, "labente dextera gladium vix trementibus digitis circuibat."

APPENDIX.

THE SHORTER LATIN ACTS OF THE MARTYRDOM OF PERPETUA AND FELICITAS[1].

FACTA persecutione sub Valeriano et Gallieno consulibus, comprehensi sunt venerabiles viri iuvenes Saturus et Saturninus, duo fratres, Revocatus et Felicitas soror eius et Perpetua quae erat de nobili genere et habebat patrem et matrem et duos fratres et filium ad mamillam. Annorum enim erat illa duorum et viginti, apud Africam in civitate Zabarbitanorum.

Minutius proconsul dixit ad eos: "Invictissimi principes Valerianus et Gallienus iusserunt ut sacrificetis."

Saturus respondit: "Hoc non sumus facturi, Christiani enim sumus."

Proconsul iussit eos recludi in carcerem; siquidem hora erat prope tertia.

Audiens vero pater Perpetuae eam esse comprehensam cucurrit ad carcerem et videns eam dixit: "Quid hoc fecisti, filia, dehonestasti enim generationem tuam. Nunquam enim de genere nostro aliquis missus est in carcerem."

Perpetua vero dixit ad eum: "Pater, ecce, verbi gratia, vides vas iacens aut fictile aut cuiuslibet generis?"

Et ille respondit: "Video, quid ad haec?"

Perpetua dixit: "Numquid aliud nomen potest habere quam quod est?"

At ille respondit: "Non."

Perpetua dixit: "Nec ego aliud nomen accipere possum quam quod sum Christiana." Tunc pater eius audito verbo irruit super eam, volens oculos eius eruere; et exclamans, confusus, egressus est foras.

Orantes vero et sine cessatione preces ad Deum effundentes, cum

---

[1] As given by Aubé from the MSS. 5269, 5279, 5292, 5297, 5311, 5318, 5349, of the National Library at Paris.

essent multis diebus in carcere, quadam nocte videns visum sancta Perpetua, alia die retulit commartyribus suis ita dicens:

"Vidi in visu hac nocte scalam erectam mirabili altitudine usque ad caelum, et ita erat angusta ut nonnisi unus per eam ascendere posset. Dextra vero laevaque inerant fixi cultri et gladii ferrei ut nullus circa se nisi ad coelum respicere posset. Sub ea vero iacebat latens draco teterrimus ingenti forma, ut prae metu eius quivis ascendere formidaret. Vidi etiam ascendentem per eam Saturum usque ad sursum et respicientem ad nos et dicentem: ne vereamini hunc draconem qui iacet; confortamini in gratia Christi, ascendite et nolite timere ut mecum partem habere possitis. Vidi etiam iuxta scalam hortum ingentem, copiosissimum et amoenum et in medio horto sedentem senem in habitu pastorali et mulgentem oves et in gyro eius stantem multitudinem candidatorum: et aspiciens ad nos vocavit ad se et dedit nobis omnibus de fructu lactis. Et cum gustassemus, turba candidatorum responderunt "Amen" et sic prae clamore vocum sum expergefacta."

At vero illi cum haec audissent gratias agentes insufficienter domino cognoverunt ex revelatione beatissimae Perpetuae ad martyrii coronam dignos esse effectos.

Post haec vero procedens Minutius proconsul et sedens pro tribunali eos exhiberi praecepit dixitque ad eos: "Sacrificate diis, sic enim iusserunt perpetui principes."

Saturus respondit: "Deo magis oportet sacrificare quam idolis."

Proconsul dixit: "Pro te respondes, aut pro omnibus?"

Saturus dixit: "Pro omnibus, una enim est in nobis voluntas."

Proconsul ad Saturninum, Revocatum, Felicitatem et Perpetuam dixit: "Vos quid dicitis?"

At illi responderunt: "Verum est, unam gerimus voluntatem."

Proconsul iussit viros a mulieribus separari et ad Saturum dixit: "Sacrifica, iuvenis, et ne te meliorem quam principes iudices esse."

Saturus respondit: "Meliorem me iudico apud verum principem et praesentis et futuri saeculi, si colluctando pati meruero."

Proconsul dixit: "Suade tibi, et sacrifica, iuvenis."

Saturus respondit: "Hoc ego non sum facturus."

Proconsul ad Saturninum dixit: "Sacrifica vel tu, iuvenis, ut valeas vivere."

Saturninus respondit: "Christianus sum et hoc mihi facere non licet."

Proconsul ad Revocatum dixit: "Forte et tu sequeris voluntatem illorum."

Revocatus respondit: "Eorum plane propter Deum sequor desideria."

Proconsul dixit: "Sacrificate ne vos interficiam."

Revocatus respondit: "Deum oramus ut hoc mereamur."

Proconsul eos removeri praecepit et Felicitatem et Perpetuam sibi iussit offerri. Dixit autem ad Felicitatem: "Quae diceris?"

Respondit: "Felicitas."

Proconsul dixit: "Virum habes?"

Felicitas respondit: "Habeo quem nunc contemno."

Proconsul dixit: "Ubi est?"

Felicitas dixit: "Non est hic."

Proconsul dixit: "Quo genere est?"

Felicitas respondit: "Plebeius."

Proconsul dixit: "Parente(s) habes?"

Felicitas dixit: "Non habeo: Revocatus vero congermanus meus est. Verumtamen his maiores parentes habere non potero."

Proconsul dixit: "Miserere tui, puella, et sacrifica ut vivas, maxime quia te infantem in utero habere video."

Felicitas respondit: "Ego Christiana sum et haec omnia mihi propter Deum contemnere praecepta sunt."

Proconsul dixit: "Consule tibi, doleo enim de te."

Felicitas respondit: "Fac quod vis, mihi enim persuadere non poteris."

Proconsul ad Perpetuam dixit: "Quid dicis, Perpetua, sacrificas?"

Perpetua, "Christiana, inquit, sum et nominis mei sequor auctoritatem, ut sim perpetua."

Proconsul dixit: "Parentes habes?"

Perpetua respondit: "Habeo."

Audientes vero parentes eius pater, mater, fratres, et maritus simulque cum parvulo eius qui erat ad lac venerunt cum essent de nobili genere. Et videns eam pater eius stantem ante proconsulis tribunal cadens in faciem suam dixit ad eam: "Filia, iam non filia, sed domina, miserere aetati meae patris tui, si tamen mereor dici pater, miserere et matris tuae, quae te ad talem florem aetatis perduxit, miserere et fratribus tuis, et huic infelicissimo viro tuo, certe vel parvulo huic qui post te vivere non poterit. Depone hanc cogitationem tuam. Nemo enim nostrum post te vivere poterit, quia hoc generi meo nunquam contigit."

Perpetua vero stabat immobilis et respiciens in caelum dixit ad patrem suum: "Pater, noli vereri, Perpetuam enim filiam tuam, si non obstiteris, perpetuam filiam tuam possidebis."

Proconsul dixit: "Moveant te et excitent ad dolorem lacrymae parentum tuorum, praeterea voces parvuli tui."

Perpetua dixit: "Movebunt me lacrymae eorum, si a conspectu domini et a consortio horum sanctorum, cum quibus secundum visionem meam fratribus bonis sum copulata, fuero aliena inventa."

Pater vero iactans infantem in collum eius et ipse cum matre et marito tenentes manus eius et flentes osculabantur dicentes: "Miserere nostri, filia, et vive nobiscum." At illa prospiciens infantem eosque repellens dixit: "Recedite a me operarii iniquitatis, quia non novi vos. Non enim potero maiores et meliores vos facere quam deum qui me ad hanc gloriam perducere dignatus est."

Videns vero proconsul eorum perseverantiam, data sententia Saturum, Saturninum et Revocatum flagellis caesos, et Perpetuam et Felicitatem exalapatas in carcerem recipi praecepit ut in Caesaris natale bestiis mitterentur.

Et cum essent in carcere iterum vidit visionem Perpetua Aegyptium quemdam horridum et nigrum iacentem et volutantem se sub pedibus eorum, retulitque sanctis fratribus et commartyribus suis. At illi intelligentes, gratias egerunt domino, qui, prostrato inimico generis humani, eos laude martyrii dignos habuerit.

Contristantibus vero iis de Felicitate quod esset praegnans in mensibus octo, statuerunt unanimiter pro ea precem ad Dominum fundere. Et dum orarent subito enixa est vivum. Quidam vero de custodibus dixit ad eam: "Quid factura es cum veneris in amphitheatrum quae talibus detineris tormentis?"

Felicitas respondit: "Hic ego crucior, ibi vero pro me Dominus patietur."

Facto itaque die natali Caesaris concursus ingens fiebat populi in amphitheatrum ad spectaculum eorum.

Procedente vero proconsule eos ad amphitheatrum perduci praecepit. Euntibus vero eis sequebatur Felicitas quae ex sanguine carnis ad salutem sanguinis ducebatur et de obstetrice ad gladium et de lavatione post partum balnei sanguinis effusione meruit delavari.

Adclamante vero turba positi sunt in medio amphitheatri nudi, ligatis post tergum manibus, et dimissis bestiis diversis, Saturus et Perpetua a leonibus sunt devorati. Saturninus vero ab ursis erutus gladio est percussus. Revocatus vero et Felicitas a leopardis gloriosum agonem impleverunt.

Horum ergo famosissimorum et beatissimorum Martyrum, sanctissimi fratres, qui passi sunt sub Valeriano et Gallieno imperatoribus apud Africam in Civitate Zabarbitanorum sub Minutio proconsule die nonarum Martiarum fideliter memoriis communicantes actus eorum in ecclesia ad edificationem legite, precantes Dei misericordiam ut orationibus eorum et omnium sanctorum nostri misereatur, atque participes eorum efficere dignetur in gloriam et laudem nominis sui quod est benedictum in saecula saeculorum. Amen.

Cambridge:
PRINTED BY C. J. CLAY, M.A. AND SONS,
AT THE UNIVERSITY PRESS.